W9-CDF-906

What every Canadian should know about

MUTUAL FUNDS

CANADIAN
SECURITIES
INSTITUTE

Toronto • Montreal • Calgary • Vancouver

All rights reserved. No part of this publication may be reproduced, stored in a retrieval system, or transmitted, in any form or by any means, electronic, mechanical, photocopying, recording, or otherwise, without prior written permission of the publisher.

Names of individual securities mentioned in this text are for purposes of example only and are not to be construed as recommendations for purchase or sale.

Prices of individual securities given in this text are for the purposes of comparison and illustration only and were approximate figures for the period when the text was being prepared. Current quotations may be obtained from the financial pages of daily newspapers, the financial press or from your Investment Advisor.

While information contained in this text has been obtained from sources the publisher believes to be reliable, it cannot be guaranteed nor does it purport to treat each subject exhaustively.

This publication is designed to provide accurate and authoritative information in regard to the subjects covered. It is distributed with the understanding that the Canadian Securities Institute and the Investor Learning Centre of Canada are not engaged in rendering legal, accounting or other professional service. If legal advice or other expert assistance is required, the services of competent professional persons should be sought.

Credits
Managing editor: Dominic Jones
Writing: Paul Irwin, Dominic Jones, Elaine Wyatt and June Yee
Design: Bowness & Yolleck Communications

CANADIAN
SECURITIES
INSTITUTE

121 King Street West
Suite 1550
Toronto, Ontario
M5H 3T9

Tel: 416-364-9130
Fax: 416-359-0486

Canadian Cataloguing in Publication Data
Main entry under title:
What every Canadian should know about mutual funds
ISBN 1-894289-06-4
1. Mutual funds.   I. Canadian Securities Institute
HG4530.W427 1999   332.63'27   C98-932912-7
First Printing 1999 by the Canadian Securities Institute
Copyright 1999 © the Canadian Securities Institute
Printed and bound in Canada by Key Interactive Inc. a Dollco Communications Co.

Making sense of investing

Now it's easier for you to become a better investor! This average-level book is suitable if you already know the basics but want to expand your knowledge to a semi-professional level.

The Investor Learning Centre of Canada (ILC) is an independent not-for-profit organization dedicated to providing quality investment information to Canadians. It was established in 1996 by the Canadian Securities Institute, the national educator for the securities industry.

The ILC offers books, seminars, resource centres and Internet services across Canada.

Chapter 1 — Mutual Fund Mania

Chapter 2 — Investments And Your Objectives   12

Chapter 3 — The Rules Of The Game 34

Chapter 4 — Death, Taxes And Mutual Fund Fees 56

Chapter 5 — Navigating
The Fund Universe 76

Chapter 6 — Fund Managers' Styles

Chapter 7 — The Art Of Fund Selection

Chapter 8 — How To Build Your Portfolio   170

Chapter 9 — Alternatives To Mutual Funds — 188

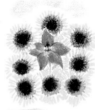

1

Mutual
Fund
Mania

With all their many advantages it's easy to see why mutual funds have become the investment of choice for Canadians.

And then there were mutual funds

Almost from out of nowhere, mutual funds have mushroomed into the investment of choice for millions of ordinary Canadians. In fact, it's estimated that around 2002, Canadians will have more invested in mutual funds than in chequing accounts, savings accounts and guaranteed investment certificates (GICs) combined. That's an astonishing statistic when you think that mutual funds were almost unheard of 15 years ago. Clearly, mutual funds are the biggest thing to hit the investment landscape in Canada in the past 50 years.

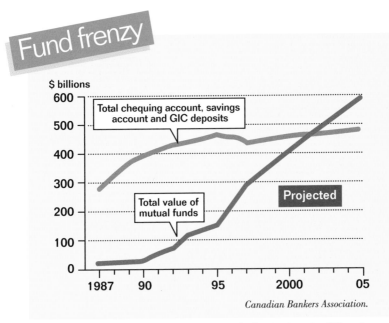

Fund frenzy

$ billions

Total chequing account, savings account and GIC deposits

Total value of mutual funds

Projected

1987　90　95　2000　05

Canadian Bankers Association.

There will soon be more money in funds than traditional investments like GICs.

Standard deviation: *Measures how volatile a fund was over a past period to give an indication of how it might behave in future.*

And yet, despite the reams of information published about them, few Canadians can confidently claim they fully understand the mutual funds in which they have invested their hard-earned savings. Survey after survey shows that we are really quite misinformed about the fund industry and its products. Indeed, a recent survey by the Canadian Bankers Association showed that 28% of us still falsely believe that our mutual funds are guaranteed. That might not seem like a high percentage, but it's alarming when you consider that not being guaranteed is the very first thing you should understand about mutual funds. You can imagine then, how few of us know what we paid last year in management fees, or know what the term *standard deviation* means.

That's the purpose of *What Every Canadian Should Know About Mutual Funds.* To give you a no-holds-barred account of mutual funds in clear and straightforward language. With this book, you should be able to build your wealth with confidence and intelligence. We will show you what mutual funds are, how they work and how to select the best and most suitable mutual funds for your portfolio. By spending some time now to gain a clear understanding of mutual funds, you will potentially save yourself a lot of grief further down the line.

What is a mutual fund?

A mutual fund is basically a pool of cash and investments managed by a professional fund manager. The fund manager buys and sells investments that fit the fund's objectives. These objectives vary from fund to fund. They may include investing in different types or classes of investments, only one class of investment or even investments from a single country or industry.

The money in the pool is gathered by the company that establishes or sponsors the fund through the sale of shares or units to investors. The fund sponsor could be a bank, trust company, mutual fund company or a life insurance firm. Each unit the fund sponsor sells represents a fraction of every investment in the fund's portfolio. In other words, each fund unit is a miniature of the full portfolio.

Investment class:
A group of investments that display common traits such as stocks, bonds or real estate.

How mutual funds work

Investor's Money   **Investor's Money**   **Investor's Money**

Fund Managers Select Investments

Investment   **Investment**   **Investment**

Profits From Investments

The value of each unit fluctuates with changes in the value of the fund's portfolio. If the portfolio rises in value, your unit's value also rises; if the portfolio falls in value, your unit's value will also fall. The value of your fund unit is called the net asset value per share (NAVPS). You calculate it by dividing the fund portfolio's total value each day by the total units the fund has issued. If the fund's portfolio is worth $100,000 and there are 100,000 units outstanding, then the NAVPS is $1 ($100,000 ÷ 100,000 units).

NAVPS:
Net asset value per share; the price of each of your fund units.

The many advantages of mutual funds

It's not for nothing that mutual funds have become the favored investment of Canadians today. They offer many unique benefits to small investors that might not otherwise be achievable. In fact, whether you have $100 to invest or $1 million, you get the same benefits from investing in funds. Here's a list of some of the key advantages:

Instant diversification

You know the old adage "Never put all your eggs in one basket." Well, when you buy into a mutual fund your money is being spread over a portfolio of many different securities. This means both your returns and risks will be tempered by this diversity, rather than tossed about by the fortunes of any single investment.

Diversification:
Spreading your money over a number of investments to reduce risk.

Many investors can find diversification difficult to achieve by themselves. Effective diversification requires a healthy pool of money. Stocks are most often sold in blocks of 100 shares, which means that an investment in a solid company can cost well over $3,000 or $4,000. At the same time, many bonds are sold in $5,000 blocks. And you would likely need at least five or 10 stocks for a diversified holding of stocks and probably a few bonds to diversify your fixed-income holdings. Meeting these investment requirements might make it hard for smaller investors to have more than a few different holdings in their portfolios. On the other hand, a stock fund may hold 100 or so stocks in 15 to 20 industries. A bond fund could hold dozens of different bonds from several issuers.

Access to global markets
Investing internationally further diversifies your portfolio. But investing in individual securities of foreign countries can be an expensive and time-consuming proposition for  individual investors. With mutual funds, though, you have a relatively cost-effective way to invest internationally. Many mutual funds today invest exclusively in securities from different regions of the world, or even in the securities of a single country. These funds are often managed by experts

who are familiar with the international markets in a way that the average investor could never be.

Easy access to your money

You can redeem your fund units at any time for what they're worth — the market or net asset value — on the day they are presented for redemption, or on the next business day. Fund companies then have five business days to pay you your money. Most funds try to pay more rapidly.

Redeem:
Sell your units back to the mutual fund company for cash.

Purchase and withdrawal plans

The mutual fund industry has also made it easy for you to buy and sell mutual funds. They have created many purchase and withdrawal plans.

There are two types of purchase plans. The first lets you invest differing or set amounts at whatever intervals you want after making a minimum initial investment. In the second plan type, called a contractual plan, you agree to buy a set dollar amount of fund units at regular intervals, usually monthly, over a defined period of years. You can cancel the plan at any time, although there is usually a fee to do so. Contractual plans are less popular because many people don't like locking themselves into a rigid savings plan.

With both plans, you can choose to be paid your capital gains, dividends or interest at the end of every month, or you can compound your returns by reinvesting them in more units of the fund. Many fund companies offer plans that let you make regular withdrawals to match your income needs.

Contract-ual plan:
When you commit to buy a set dollar amount of fund units regularly over a period of years.

Flexible amounts

Most fund companies accept initial purchases of
$50 to $1,000. After your first purchase you can
choose to invest as little as $10 every month or so.
Many people arrange for automatic monthly
withdrawals from their bank accounts to be put into
funds. This is a convenient and painless forced
savings method.

Contributing regular amounts also lets you
take advantage of dollar cost averaging. This is
when you regularly invest a set amount of money in
the fund and get more units when the net asset
value has fallen, and fewer units when the net asset
value has risen. Over the long term, dollar cost
averaging may reduce the average price you pay for
your fund units. See chart opposite.

Professional management

Each mutual fund is run by one or more investment
professionals called fund or portfolio managers.
Often backed by a research team, the fund
manager continuously monitors the fund's portfolio
and the general investment climate. Most fund
managers may have many years of experience and
advanced academic qualifications that enable them
to make informed investment decisions. They
devote many hours to researching the economy, the
markets and individual securities before making an
investment.

In essence, the thousands of individual
contributors to the fund are collectively hiring the
fund manager. While the service you get in a fund

**Research
team:**
*A group of
investment
analysts
who help
the fund
manager
assess
which
investments
to buy.*

Installment buying

How dollar cost averaging works

Months	1	2	3	4	5	6	7
Monthly unit value	$2.35	$2.80	$3.00	$2.30	$1.60	$1.00	$0.90
Units you get for $100	42.55	35.71	33.33	43.48	62.50	100.00	111.11
Your average cost per unit	$2.35	$2.55	$2.69	$2.58	$2.30	$1.89	$1.63
Average market price per unit	$2.35	$2.58	$2.72	$2.61	$2.41	$2.18	$1.99

After seven months in this example, your $1.63 average purchase price is 18% less than the $1.99 average market price.

isn't tailored to your specific needs as it would be if you had your own private investment manager, the benefits are similar. Professional management relieves you of the time, resources and responsibility of managing the individual investments yourself. Instead, you can simply focus on the less complicated task of ensuring a fund's objectives continue to fit your own.

Professional investment management is also important if you're interested in small market niches, such as an industry sector or a particular country. Instead of having to become expert in all types of investments, you can buy units of a fund managed by someone who already has the unique expertise you're looking for. Many international funds are run by managers who live in the regions they invest in. This gives them unique insights into these markets, something that cannot easily be duplicated from afar.

Another benefit of mutual funds is that the investments they contain will continue to be managed after your death and while your estate is in probate. However, like other kinds of securities, mutual funds cannot be readily traded during probate.

Ironically, professional management is a double-edge sword. It can also be one of the potential disadvantages of investing in mutual funds.

Probate:
The legal process to divide your property after your death.

Disadvantages of mutual funds

Sales and management fees

Redemption charge:
Fee you pay when you sell a fund, usually higher for short-term investment.

Fees associated with mutual fund investing can be high, particularly if you use a fund to park your money for a short period and are hit with redemption charges when you cash out. If you are prepared to spend the time needed to pick individual stocks and bonds — rather than hold those investments indirectly through mutual funds — you can end up spending less in fees. This would be the case particularly if you didn't trade your investments often. You would typically pay sales commissions when you buy and sell stocks and bonds, but not the on-going management fees that are part of the package when you buy mutual funds. Mutual fund fees are discussed at length in Chapter 4.

Some loss of control

Hand-in-hand with the professional money management you get with a mutual fund comes the loss of all control over your investment except the right to sell it. Although you usually choose a fund for its ability to match your investment objectives, you do not have a say in what the fund buys or sells at any given time. The fund's investments are tailored to a large group of investors, not to your personal feelings about a certain security or market. Remember, security selection is the job of the manager and the investment team.

It's also important to remember that, as good as a manager might be, nobody is infallible. The performance of most mutual funds reflects trends in the market, enhanced by the decisions of the portfolio manager. But sometimes they make mistakes. There is not a money manager in Canada who will always deliver superior results. In fact, most funds don't beat the markets they invest in.

Security:
A general term to describe all kinds of investments.

No guarantee of return
Often overlooked, this is an important disadvantage for people accustomed to the guaranteed return on common bank investments like GICs or Canada Savings Bonds (CSBs). A mutual fund's unit price fluctuates along with the value of the investments in the portfolio. There is no telling what a fund's unit price will be at any future date, and the risk of losing money is a real possibility.

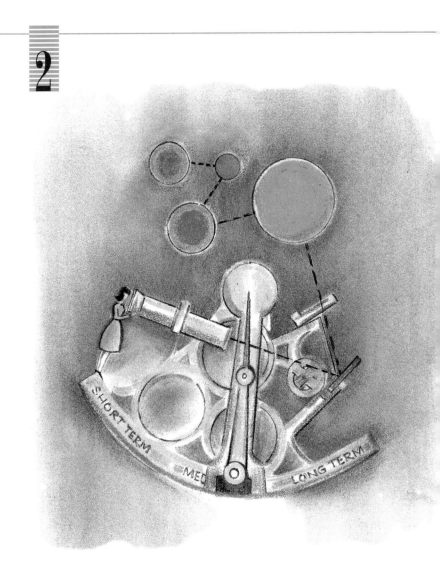

Investments
and your
Objectives

On the surface, mutual funds can seem deceptively simple. But before you leap into the mutual funds craze yourself, know what you're buying.

How much research would you do if you were going to entrust your life savings to a handful of stocks? Now ask yourself this: did you spend the same amount of time researching the mutual funds you own? Most likely you didn't. Most of us do nowhere near enough research before we buy a fund. Perhaps this lack of due diligence has something to do with the misconception that mutual funds are somehow different than stocks and bonds, or at the very least that they are nowhere near as risky as the individual investments.

Many people do a second take when they hear that a number of mutual funds have proven to be riskier than some individual stocks. What's more, still others seem oblivious to the fact that most funds are in fact made up of individual stocks and bonds, which in turn are subject to the vagaries of the market. Maybe this lack of awareness has something to do with the ease with which you can buy mutual funds. At the same place you once bought GICs and CSBs promising to pay back at least what you put in, you can now buy mutual funds that invest in the stock market with no guarantee. Some long-time financial institution clients don't realize the difference. In fact, almost a third of Canadians think mutual funds are guaranteed.

Even if you do understand this distinction, the point is that mutual funds' mass market appeal gives them a deceptive aura of simplicity. They are, however, more complicated than individual securities in many ways. To properly understand them, you need two levels of understanding.

First, you need a basic knowledge of the nature of the individual securities in a fund. And then you

Risk quiz

What percentage of Canadian stock mutual funds were found to be riskier than 35 of the biggest companies listed on the Toronto Stock Exchange?

a) 10%
b) 20%
c) 30%
d) 40%

Answer: d. 40%*

*Based on 3-year standard deviation at July '98 on TSE 35 index vs. same measure of all Canadian equity funds using PALTrak mutual fund analysis software.

need to understand how the fund itself is put together and managed.

While most of this book explains the second level of understanding, you cannot properly understand mutual funds unless you understand the investments in them. While you're not expected to become an expert on picking stocks, bonds or treasury bills — that's the fund manager's job — you should at least know what their risks are and how the fund earns a return on them.

Understanding the three asset classes

Most investments can be separated into one of three major groups called asset classes. The investments in each asset class have similar origins and characteristics. The three main asset classes are:

• Cash and cash equivalents;
• Fixed-income securities; and,
• Equities.

When you understand the nature of each of these asset classes, you are better able to select mutual funds that fit your requirements. That's because mutual funds will either hold investments from one asset class or a combination of each.

Cash and cash equivalent investments
These investments include the money you keep in the bank. Also included are common investments like GICs and CSBs. GICs and CSBs are considered the same as cash because you can, in

T-bill:
Safe investment of less than one year issued by governments and sold to investors in blocks of $1 million or more.

Corporate paper:
Similar to T-bills above but sold by companies.

many cases, get your money back at any time. They're as good as, or equivalent to, cash.

The most common cash and cash equivalent investments that mutual funds buy are Government of Canada treasury bills (T-bills) and company corporate paper. Both of these are short-term investments of less than one year.

When you buy a T-bill or corporate paper, you are lending money to the issuing government or company. The government borrows a lot of money for short periods to tide it over between when it spends money and when it gets in money through taxes. Companies borrow for short periods to cover expenses until they receive payment for the goods they've produced or the services they've provided.

T-bills and corporate paper are considered as good as cash because of their short duration. The risks of lending your money to a company or government over a period of months are generally less than over several years. There's less chance of something going wrong over the short term, which means you have a higher chance of getting your money back. Because of this, the value of these investments stays quite stable.

However, of the two, T-bills are often safer than corporate paper. They're backed by governments, which have the power to get money through taxes. Companies don't have that luxury. They get money by selling their products and services at a profit. Since many things can affect a firm's profitability, short-term corporate borrowings are generally riskier than T-bills.

Since cash and cash equivalents are typically the safest investments, you cannot expect to earn a high return on them. Returns between different types of cash or cash equivalents will vary slightly, depending on the length of their term and the issuer's creditworthiness. The longer the term, the higher the return typically is. The higher the risk of the issuer being unable to repay the loan, the higher the typical return. Investors who buy cash and equivalent investments want safety for their money.

Returns from cash and cash equivalents come in one of two ways. GICs and CSBs pay you interest periodically. Others such as T-bills and corporate paper are sold for less than their maturity value. They may be sold to you for $990 and mature three months later for $1,000, giving you a $10 gain. However, the gain is translated into an annual percentage so you can compare the return to other investments. The gain is also treated as interest for income tax purposes, which is taxed at the highest rate.

Term:
The time until an investment matures or a loan has to be repaid.

Creditworthiness:
A borrower's track record and current and future financial ability to live up to a loan's requirements.

Fixed-income investments

There are two main types of fixed-income investments – bonds and preferred shares. When governments and companies want to borrow for periods of more than a year, they often issue bonds or debentures to a number of lenders. These lenders are then free to sell the bonds or debentures to other investors on the bond market.

Each bond or debenture details the terms of the original loan, such as the amount borrowed (the principal), when the loan will be repaid (the maturity date) and the fixed rate of interest to be paid (the coupon rate). The certificate will also detail what, if any, assets the issuer is putting up as collateral for the loan. If there are specific assets pledged, then the loan is a bond. If the loan isn't secured by assets, then it's a debenture.

Bonds are considered safer than debentures because they're backed by assets. If the issuer fails to pay interest or repay the loan, then bondholders can use the assets to recover their money. With debentures, there are no assets to sell. Government bonds are really debentures, but they're called bonds because of governments' unique power to raise money through taxes, providing bond-like security.

A number of other factors determine the risk level of bonds and debentures. Government bonds are almost always viewed as safer than company bonds or debentures. Shorter-term bonds and debentures are generally safer than longer-term ones because there's less chance for something to go wrong over the bond's life. Similarly, bonds and debentures that pay higher rates of interest are typically safer than those with lower coupons. That's because a higher interest-paying bond pays you more of your return earlier in the bond's term than one with a lower coupon rate.

Preferred shares are not bonds, but they have

Maturity value:
The amount of money returned to the lender when a loan comes due.

Issuer:
A government or company that issues bonds or shares.

Years in which bonds have done better than stocks

Year	Stocks*	Long-term Bonds+
1998		B
1997		B
1996	S	
1995		B
1994	S	
1993	S	
1992		B
1991		B
1990		B
TOTAL	**3**	**6**

*TSE 300 index
+ScotiaMcLeod Long-term bond index

While stocks do better over the long haul, bonds can outperform in particular years.

similar characteristics. Just as most bonds pay a fixed amount of interest, preferreds generally pay a set amount of dividends. Dividends are a payment out of a company's profits. A company must meet all its debt obligations — including bond interest — before it can pay dividends. This means dividends from preferreds are less certain than bond interest payments. In fact, a company doesn't have to pay dividends. However, if it does, then preferred shareholders have a prior claim on the dividends ahead of common shareholders. A major attraction of investing in preferreds is that Revenue Canada offers a tax break on dividends of most Canadian public companies. Depending on your income level, this can mean dividends are taxed the least.

Principal:
The original amount of a loan or the amount you put into an investment.

Interest rates:
The current amount charged to borrow money for different lengths of time; usually influenced by changes in inflation.

Inflation:
An increase in prices of goods and services which reduces how much you can buy for your dollar.

Besides the regular interest or dividend payments you get investing in bonds and preferred shares, you can also get a capital gain. A capital gain is when you sell an investment for more than you paid. This happens with bonds and preferreds primarily when interest rates go down after you've bought the investment. When interest rates fall, bond and preferred share prices go up. The opposite happens when interest rates rise; bond and preferred share prices go down.

Prices on bonds and preferreds fluctuate to keep pace with the rates of interest being paid on similar new investments. These price changes don't affect the amount of interest or dividends you get because these are fixed when the securities are first issued. But a bond that pays 5% interest will sell in the bond market for less than similar new bonds that are paying 6%. The discount on the 5% bond compensates for the lower rate of interest and gives the buyer a profit when the bond matures. This profit pushes up the buyer's return to around 6%. If you decided instead to buy the 6% bond and interest rates went down to 5%, you would be able to sell your bond for more than you paid. The buyer would realize a loss when the bond matured, reducing the return to around 5% from 6%. This mix of capital gain or loss plus the stream of set interest or dividend payments gives you a total return that's known as the yield to maturity.

These price fluctuations are why interest rate changes are so important to the returns on a bond fund. When interest rates drop – usually because of falling inflation — a bond fund will do well. When rates are ratcheting up – because of rising inflation — bond funds will perform poorly. The impact of interest rates is more pronounced on longer-term bonds, those with low coupon rates and bonds of low quality issuers. In other words, if you think general interest rates are set to drop, then you will buy a fund that holds mostly long-term, low-coupon bonds from higher risk issuers to maximize your potential return. Of course, if rates don't drop, or even rise, you could face a significant loss.

Equities – ownership securities

Equities are ownership investments such as common stock. Instead of lending money to a company, you buy a piece of a business and get to share in the company's profits and future prospects.

Compared to cash and cash equivalents and fixed-income securities, equities are riskier. As one of the business' owners, you only have a claim to the money left over after the company has paid all its expenses, debts and preferred dividends. If you own shares in a company that isn't generating a lot of profit, there could very well be nothing for you to share in. Also, if the firm goes bankrupt, common shareholders have last claim on the business' assets, which often is little or nothing.

You can earn a return on common stock in two ways: through dividend payments out of the company's profits, or through capital gains if the company's shares become more valuable because it

Common share- holder:
A part owner of a company who benefits only from what is left in the firm after all debts and liabilities have been paid.

Dividend:
A provisional payment to you out of a company's profits, usually paid quarterly.

is successful. Dividends are uncertain and the company is not obliged to pay them. However, many companies have consistently paid dividends for many years. The board of directors can decide to reinvest profits back into the business to finance its growth. The thinking is that shareholders can benefit from this strategy if the company grows and generates higher profits. This will make the company's shares more valuable. If you sell your shares, you could realize a capital gain. Capital gains get favorable tax treatment. You only have to pay tax on three-quarters of the gain.

Capital gain:
The profit you make when you sell something for more than you paid.

Historically, equities have earned higher returns over the long-term than the other two asset classes. However, they are more volatile over the short-term and can fluctuate widely in daily trading. Over a period of 10 or 15 years, these fluctuations generally even out to an above-average return.

All stocks are not the same, though. There's a wide range of them, each with different potential risks and returns. A big, profitable company that pays dividends is obviously different than a small venture that has no profit but which is developing a potential cure for cancer. While it's hard to say which is the better investment, the profitable dividend paying company is less risky. The chances of this company going out of business are less than for the small biotechnology firm. Of course, if the small firm succeeds in finding the cancer cure, its shares could rise dramatically on its prospects for potentially huge future profits. But the risk is dire if it fails in its quest and goes bankrupt.

An important concept to understand about stocks is that the price of a share represents the value put on it by investors. But the price doesn't tell you whether the company has high or low earnings. A company that is making money, but less than investors expected, could see its stock price fall substantially. And another firm, that has yet to make any money, might command a higher stock price because investors have bid its price up on the belief it will have big earnings.

To grow your money you will have to look to the stock market.

You can get an idea of the risk of a stock by looking at how much profit or earnings the company is generating for each share that it has issued. A share that is trading for $100 may be that of a company that earned $5 in profit for every share investors own. This means the share price is 20 times earnings ($100 divided by $5). A $1 stock may have only one cent of earnings behind it, which means it is trading at 100 times earnings ($1 divided by one cent). In terms of value, the $100 stock is more attractive — and probably less risky — because it's backed by more earnings, money that might be paid out to you as dividends or reinvested in the business.

Earnings:
Another word for a company's profits; also called net earnings.

Market cap:
The total market value of all the shares of a company that investors own.

A stock term you will often find used in mutual fund literature is "cap" or market cap, as used in large-cap, mid-cap or small-cap. This refers to a company's market capitalization, the total value of all the company's shares that investors own. A company with 10 million issued shares, each trading for $5, will have a market capitalization of $50 million (10 million shares multiplied by $5 per share). In mutual funds, a large-cap company in Canada is generally one with a market capitalization of more than $3 billion. In the U.S., the cut-off is generally U.S. $6 billion.

The trade-off between risk and return

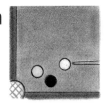

When you think about it, investing really comes down to the relationship between risk and return. The rule of thumb is that higher returns come with higher risk. Of course, the get-rich-quick bent in the human condition prompts most of us to focus more on an investment's potential returns than on the perils inherent in getting them. To become truly comfortable with the risks you are taking with your investments, you need to understand more clearly the types of risk that can affect your investing success. Risk describes the various possible factors that can cause either a price decline in an investment or a failure to provide the expected income. Here are some of the key risks you face:

Buying power: *To increase your dollar's buying power your return must be higher than the inflation rate.*

• **Liquidity risk:** This is the risk that you won't

be able to sell your investment quickly and easily and, get a reasonable price. Many investments can't be cashed at the issuer and must be sold on the open market. If there isn't a ready market for the investment, you won't get a good price for it.

Liquidity: *How easily you can sell an investment on the market and get a good price.*

- **Credit risk:** The underlying issue in credit risk is the soundness of the corporation issuing the security. For fixed-income and equity instruments, this may mean the issuer should have enough earnings to pay interest and dividends over the life of the investment.

- **Inflation or buying power risk:** It's natural to want to get back at least what you originally invested. For conservative investors, investments that pay a prescribed rate of interest as well as guaranteeing the original investment may seem to carry no risk. However, no investment is truly risk-free. If the return on your investment is less than inflation, then you are poorer than when you started. You have lost part of your buying power because inflation has pushed up prices for the things you need to buy. If you're not growing your money at a higher rate than inflation, then you are "going broke safely."

- **Market risk:** All investments are susceptible to market risk all the time. No matter how high the quality of the issuer or meticulous the selection process, most security prices follow general market trends.

- **Exchange rate or currency risk:** This risk

Monetary policy: *Government action taken to boost or slow economic growth by influencing interest rates.*

Nationalize: *When a government seizes private property, sometimes with little, if any, compensation to the owners.*

stems from the fact that many domestic corporations do business globally. While you may have invested in a Canadian-based company whose earnings are calculated in Canadian dollars, the corporation's operations or sales could be in a variety of overseas countries. Depending on the strength of the Canadian dollar, profits generated in other parts of the world could be worth significantly less — or more — when exchanged into Canadian dollars. You face the same kind of risk if you invest in foreign companies and the Canadian dollar strengthens against the currencies in which they report earnings.

- **Political risk:** While the government plays a direct role in the economy by setting monetary policy, there are other indirect risks to your investments that stem from government policy. Regulatory changes in a particular industry could affect the future profitability of companies in the sector and hurt your investment in them. If you invest in the stock of a Canadian tobacco company that sells most of its product in Canada, the value of your investment would likely fall substantially if the federal government imposed heavy new sin taxes on cigarettes to discourage people from smoking. Similarly, if you own the stock of a forestry company that has to pay increased royalty fees to the province where it operates, this may cause the company's stock price to fall.

Political risk can be a significant concern for

Canadians investing abroad. Maybe you have money invested in a Canadian gold exploration company that operates in an African nation that lacks proper mining legislation. The firm may spend millions of dollars to drill for gold on promising lands, only to see the government of that country nationalize the gold find without compensation. You and anyone else who invested in the exploration company will have lost all the money that was spent looking for the gold.

Don't assume, however, that political risk is just overseas. In the lead-up to the referendum on Quebec separation in 1995, interest rates in Canada rose, creating capital losses for bond investors. Investing all of your money in just one country, even Canada, exposes you to more risk than investing in a range of countries at various stages of development.

Invest to meet your own goals

To sort out what combination of investment types you need means answering a host of questions. How much money do I have available to invest? How long am I investing for? How much growth do I need? Do I need income from my investments? How much risk am I prepared to take?

Investing can help finance your dreams

Your choice of investments, of course, must

Insider trading: *When a company insider or 10% shareholder trades a company's shares, illegal if trading is based on important confidential information.*

also recognize your individual preferences and constraints. You might have a legal or ethical reason for not investing in certain securities. If you are an officer or a member of the board of directors of a public company, you must be careful to abide by insider trading rules. For ethical reasons, you might choose not to invest in companies involved in certain countries or industries. You might have preferences driven by your background, family situation or personal interests.

If you are investing in fixed-income mutual funds, you might prefer to receive your income quarterly rather than annually. If your heirs live in the United States, you might prefer more exposure to the U.S. capital markets to protect your children's inheritance. Some investors like to invest more in gold than is usual, others are particularly interested in the development of biotechnology.

You will seldom have only one investment goal or objective. Young investors often have an eye on a distant retirement but their hearts on a home and a university education for their children. Older investors might be concerned about their income, today and tomorrow, as well as leaving something to their heirs. You should take the time to distinguish between these many goals and, if you think it makes sense, buy different mutual funds to meet each of your goals.

Of course, your objectives will change over time and you must try to respond to these changes. The birth of a child, a marriage, a divorce, a loss of job or a career change could trigger changes to

your objectives and your investment portfolio.
What should be clear is that investment goals are
like fingerprints; no two are exactly alike. However,
most people's objectives fall into one of three major
categories — growth, income or safety.

Safety

Safety is an investment objective aimed
at preserving your principal or capital.
If you are saving money that you simply
must have in a year or two – maybe for
a down payment on your dream home or
to start a business – safety will be your priority. You
might put the money in a cash-type investment like a
money market mutual fund that invests in
government treasury bills. Basically, safety means
getting all of your money back when you need it.

Income

Income is when you want your investments to generate interest or some other
kind of income. You may need this
money to live on or you might want it to
reinvest. Getting an early return on your
money is safer than waiting a long time for it. You
usually get income in the form of interest from fixed-
income securities such as bonds or as dividends from
common or preferred shares. You can achieve your
income objective by buying mutual funds that invest
in these fixed-income securities. If you are retired,
then income will likely be your main objective.

Growth

Even investors who are most interested in income will also have some need for growth in order to protect their buying power.

Another word for growth is capital appreciation. You put your money in an investment and later you get back more than you put in, what's called a capital gain. Growth is typically a longer term objective. You've got to be prepared to put your money away for a period of years and not touch it. If you have 10 years or more to go to retirement and you don't need your money before then, then growth will probably be your main objective. Equities have historically been the best growth investments over the long term.

Second-guess your risk tolerance

Many people have much less tolerance for risk than they might realize. Surveys show that 30% to 40% of us are uncomfortable about the risks we are taking with our investments. If some fears are irrational, others are due to a lack of knowledge. It's common for people to underestimate their true response until a loss actually occurs.

To better understand how you might react, look at historical returns from different investment types. This will not only make obvious the unpredictability of the markets, but you will also see how dramatically different the returns can be between investments. The TSE 300 composite index, representing 300 companies on the Toronto Stock Exchange, has historically produced an average annual return of about 10 per cent. But that average masks the ups and downs along the way. The index has given investors returns of 30% and more some years and losses of about 25% in others, sometimes over a short time.

Would a big drop like that prompt you to sell your stock mutual funds, fearing more declines are coming? Or would you invest more heavily, believing the drop was a buying opportunity? Many people panic when they see the value of their savings decline, which causes them to make irrational decisions, such as selling an investment for no other reason than a temporary slip in value. Even if you are aware that stock prices can go up and down and believe you are prepared for the turmoil, remember that you might react differently under the pressure of a major market slide.

Whether you are investing for growth or income, your tolerance for risk can force you to make compromises. You may discover the return you need on your investments can come only from investments that would bring more risk than you would like to take on. In that case, you must either learn to live with a riskier portfolio, establish goals that are more modest, or save and invest more.

To create a snapshot of your ability to tolerate

TSE 300:
This is a diverse group of 300 companies that trade on the Toronto Stock Exchange and typify the state of the country's economy.

Portfolio:
A collection of investments put together to achieve a defined objective.

How much risk are you comfortable taking?

Over short periods, most investments move up and down in value. At least to some extent, you will have an emotional reaction to these market fluctuations. Emotion leads many investors to ditch an appropriate long-term strategy. That's why you have to identify your own tolerance for risk. You need investments that you are comfortable owning.

To get you starting to think about this issue, try this simple exercise. Using the risk/return chart, mark the box that most closely matches the investment strategy that suits you. Remember that increased returns mean more risk. Then look at the corresponding portfolio to find the asset allocation that's right for you.

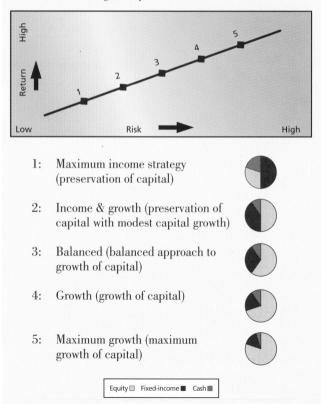

1:     Maximum income strategy (preservation of capital)

2:     Income & growth (preservation of capital with modest capital growth)

3:     Balanced (balanced approach to growth of capital)

4:     Growth (growth of capital)

5:     Maximum growth (maximum growth of capital)

Equity ▢   Fixed-income ■   Cash ■

risk, many mutual fund companies and fund sellers use a simple quiz to help you assess your risk profile. Questions often focus on your feelings or the choices you would make in life situations carrying different degrees of risk. These questions sometimes are used to try to quantify your risk tolerance by asking things that appear to have little to do with investing, but which can reveal your psychological makeup. Others can measure your risk tolerance more precisely. One of these is called the "risky alternatives" test. You are asked to express your preference for one bet over another. You might be asked to choose between Bet One in which there is an 80% probability of winning $4,000 and a 20% chance of losing $2,000, or Bet Two in which there is a 19% chance of winning $18,000 and an 81% chance of losing $1,000. If you chose Bet Two, that indicates you can tolerate more risk than the person who opts for Bet One.

Invest for the long term

Mutual funds are not designed for investors who want to trade with a hope and a prayer of getting rich quick. You can use some funds as parking places for cash or emergency reserves, but mutual funds are generally managed to produce strong returns over time. Although both bond and stock markets tend to move up and down unpredictably month-to-month or even day-to-day, it's important to realize that risk for every kind of investment diminishes over time. Remain focused on your long-term goals and the ability of each kind of investment to generate returns within the time you have available.

The Rules
of the
Game

Knowing your rights before you sit down to buy a fund could save you strife later on.

Why you simply must read this chapter

Let's face it, very few of us take the time to read the fine print before we sign a contract or agreement. In fact, it's not just legal contracts that we have an aversion to. How many of the millions of people who've played Monopoly do you think have actually read the rules cover to cover? Not very many, to be sure.

While we know we should, reading all that legal gobbledygook just seems like too much trouble. When it comes to investing, though, you have to understand the rules of the game before you start. After all, this is not a board game we're talking about. This is real life with real

money at stake. The risks and costs of not understanding your rights from the outset can be very painful indeed.

Disclosure:
The legal obligation a fund company has to inform you about the pros and cons of a fund.

Fortunately, there shouldn't be a shortage of information about a fund you might want to buy. That's because the law says fund companies must give you all the information you need to make an educated investment decision. This is called disclosure, and it's one of the fundamental principles on which Canada's investment markets operate. Under the disclosure laws, investors should have access to information that will allow them to make an informed decision about whether to buy or sell an investment.

With mutual funds, there are two key disclosure documents that you will likely encounter. The first is the so-called simplified prospectus. This is the "rule book" for investing in a fund and it should be given to you before you invest. Most often, a mutual fund company will have one simplified prospectus for all of the funds it sells.

The second disclosure document you will find is the fund's annual or semi-annual financial statements. These are a kind of "report card" on the fund's financial health. The fund firm sends these to you at least once a year.

Each of these two disclosure documents contain a huge amount of information. In a moment we will introduce you to the key information you will — and won't — find in each of these documents. We'll explain in simple language what your legal rights are as a fund investor, and what you should be wary of when someone wants to sell you a fund.

But first we should caution you that while much of what we cover here is common to most funds, there are nuances peculiar to each fund family, to each fund within a family, and even differences depending on the province in which you live. You should read the disclosure documents for each fund you want to buy. This will help ensure you pick funds that match your investment objectives.

Prospectus:
A legal document that describes a fund's investment objectives, risks and costs.

The prospectus explains the rules of the game

Normally when a company sells new investments to the public it has to file a prospectus with the provincial government securities administrators. The prospectus is a legal document that's meant to disclose all the information you need to be able to assess the investment's merits. However, once the securities have been distributed, investors are free to buy and sell them without a prospectus. A prospectus generally only needs to be filed again if the company issues new securities.

However, with mutual funds, there's an exception to this rule. Even though you are buying

Securities administrators:
Provincial government bodies charged with policing the investment business and protecting the investing public.

a freshly issued security each time you buy more fund units, mutual funds must publish and distribute a new prospectus only once a year. This replaces the need to do so for every new issue. Many mutual funds are issuing new shares to dozens, even hundreds, of new investors almost every business day. It would be impossible to publish a new prospectus for each one.

A second difference is that mutual funds can use a simplified prospectus rather than a traditional prospectus. The mutual funds salesperson must

affected by changes in interest rates.

Royal Canadian T-Bill Fund
This fund invests only in high quality, short-term debt securities, such as treasury bills, which have been issued or guaranteed by the Government of Canada. The fund intends to maintain a unit value of $10.

Royal Canadian Money Market Fund
This fund invests primarily in high quality, short-term debt securities, such as treasury bills, which have been issued or guaranteed by Canadian governments or their agencies, or bank... commercial paper

The fund's objectives must be clearly explained

give you a copy to read while you are making your decision. Reading the simplified prospectus is like kicking the tires when you buy a car.

In fact, even if you have signed an agreement to buy shares or units of a fund and put your money on the table, you might have the right to change your mind if you aren't given the prospectus. This is called your right of rescission. Because any delay in delivering the prospectus to you extends your right of rescission, it's common for it to be in your hands at the time you buy.

What the prospectus covers

The most important information in the simplified prospectus includes:

- The fund's investment objectives. While a prospectus will tell you if a fund is invested for income or capital appreciation, the objective is usually broad. This gives fund managers greater freedom to invest where they believe they will find the best returns. But it also means funds with identical objectives can be very different;

RISK FACTORS

Each Fund has its own level of risk. In general, risk is associated with fluctuations in the net asset value of a Fund. The value of a unit of a Fund is directly related to the market value of the investments it holds. Sector Funds tend to have above average risk because they focus their investments in specialized segments of the marketplace.

While we can control some risks, there are others that are beyond our control. Here's a closer look at some of those risks:

MARKET RISK Ⓜ

The market value of a Fund's investments will fluctuate according to changes in general economic and market conditions in Canada, the United States and elsewhere. Some Funds will experience greater short-term ⁿ   ⁻ than others.

Carefully read the risks for your fund.

- The types of investments that the fund can make;
- Risk factors such as the risks inherent in the markets and in individual securities, currency fluctuations, and political turmoil;

- The income tax consequences of investing in the fund;
- An explanation of your rights as an investor;
- A summary of the fees, sales charges and expenses that you must pay. We discuss these in more detail in Chapter 4. The prospectus might also include the management expense ratio (MER) for the past five years; and,
- Notice of any legal proceedings or material changes. A material change is any change that could affect the well being of the fund or fund sponsor. This could include a change in the fund's objective or if the fund is combined with another fund. Material changes are so important the prospectus must be amended when they occur, and you must receive a copy of the amendment.

MER:
A fund's expenses stated as a percentage of its assets.

Other information

The simplified prospectus must also contain the following, perhaps less pivotal, information:

TAX CONSIDERATIONS

In computing their income in each year that they hold units of the Funds as capital property, individuals resident in Canada must include the net income and net taxable capital gains payable to them by the Funds, including Management Fee Rebates, whether paid in cash or reinvested in additional units of the Funds. Generally, the character of amounts received through the Funds will be the same as if received directly by investors. Investors may realize a taxable capital gain or allowable capital loss upon a disposition of units, including a sale to transfer their investment to units of another Fund.

Taxes are usually passed on to you.

- Information documents available from the fund;
- A description of the mutual fund company's business, including an explanation of its corporate structure, as well as its management, distributors and portfolio managers;
- How the fund sets the price of the securities being sold or redeemed;
- The fund's methods for distributing shares or units;
- What dividends or other distributions you will receive;
- Who the fund's auditors, transfer agent and registrar are.

Your rights as a mutual fund investor

One of the things listed in the simplified prospectus are your rights as an investor. These are important, so it's worthwhile to look more closely at each.

Right of redemption

You have the right to redeem or sell your investment in a mutual fund at any time simply by placing a redemption order with the fund company or dealer where you hold your account. Orders to redeem are sent to the fund company's head office. Some companies require redemption instructions in writing, whether it's a letter or an order form. If the fund's NAVPS is calculated daily, most fund companies will redeem the shares the same day or on the following business day, depending on when the order is received. If the fund is valued monthly, requests for redemption may have to be sent as much as 10 days before the NAVPS is calculated.

Illiquid: *An investment that can't easily be sold for cash for a reasonable price.*

Whatever the valuation schedule, you must be paid your money within five business days after the NAVPS is calculated. The amount you get when you sell depends on the value of the shares or units. This could be more or less than you paid.

Almost all mutual funds have the right to suspend redemptions under unusual or emergency conditions. There might be a suspension if trading in 50% or more of the securities in the fund's portfolio is suspended. Historically, redemptions have rarely been suspended in Canada except among real estate funds. The illiquid nature of their holdings has made it difficult at times for these funds to fill redemptions.

Your rights as a mutual fund investor

As an investor, you have the right in some provinces to cancel your agreement to buy mutual funds:

- within two business days after receiving our simplified prospectus
- within 48 hours after receiving confirmation of your purchase
- if you don't receive our simplified prospectus
- if the prospectus contains a misrepresentation.

You may receive financial compensation in some jurisdictions if you can prove damages. There is a time limit for all claims.

Your rights must be highlighted in the prospectus.

You can change your mind

Among your rights as a mutual fund investor is the right to cancel your agreement to buy a fund under certain circumstances. If you have invested a lump sum, you have two business days after receiving the purchase confirmation, or two business days after getting the fund prospectus, to cancel the transaction.

If you have chosen to invest a certain amount of money every month or every quarter, usually through a purchase plan, you have 60 days after receiving the prospectus or confirmation to cancel your purchase.

If you don't get a simplified prospectus or if the prospectus contains a misrepresentation, you may be able to rescind your agreement to buy funds for periods of up to one year. In some cases, you may be compensated if you can show damages. However, rescissions are allowed only on amounts under the statutory limit — $50,000 in Ontario — and you must notify the dealer in writing. If you believe you have been wronged, you should consult a lawyer or your provincial securities commission.

Purchase plan:
An account where you agree to regularly invest a set dollar amount for a set period.

You can vote on what happens to your fund

Because most mutual funds are set up as investment trusts and governed by a board of trustees, individual investors are entitled to vote on material changes to the fund. These changes could include a merger, a change in the management fee, or a change in the fund's investment objectives.

Material change:
A major change that changes the nature of the fund you own.

Voting on these changes could take place at the fund's annual or a special meeting. If you can't attend, you can still vote using a proxy form that you date and sign. It lets you give the fund, or another person, the right to vote on your behalf. You mark on the form how you are voting on particular issues, and then mail it back to the fund company.

Reading a fund's financial statements

The second document in the simplified prospectus system is the annual financial statements. These statements must contain a balance sheet, income statement, statement of investment portfolio, and a statement of changes in net assets. Many funds also include a statement of portfolio transactions.

To make them more palatable for investors, you will most often get these financial statements in a bright-looking annual report, but they may also be included in the fund's prospectus. The annual report will usually include a summary about each fund in the family. This information may include historical rates of return, a summary portfolio break-down, and a profile and commentary from the fund manager. When you get the annual report, check to make sure that the management of the fund continues to match your understanding and expectations gleaned from the prospectus.

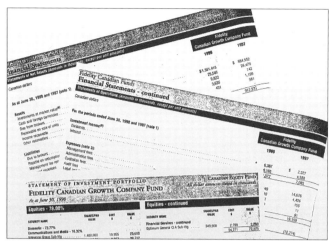

Fund's have three main financial statements.

Types of statements

At the back of the annual report, you will find the financial statements, including:

- The *balance sheet*, also called the *statement of financial position* or *the statement of net assets*, which shows the fund's assets, including the market value of investments, liabilities and equity.

- The *income statement*, also known as the *statement of operations* which details the fund's revenues and expenses. The revenue earned by most funds is interest or dividends from the securities held. A real estate fund would report rent from income properties. The management fee paid to the fund manager is often the largest expense. Other expenses include brokerage commissions, auditor's fees and administrative charges not covered by the management fee. To determine net income, expenses are deducted from the revenues.

Balance sheet:
Statement showing fund company's assets and liabilities at a point in time.

Income statement:
Shows how much a fund company's investments have earned, after paying all expenses.

Portfolio statement:
Lists what securities the fund holds.

**Maturity
date:**
*The date
that the face
value of the
bond must
be paid.*

- A *statement of investment portfolio*, also known as a *statement of investments and other net assets*. This statement gives details on the securities or other assets the fund holds. Stocks are listed with both the cost price and the market value. Bonds are listed with the cost, market value, coupon rate and maturity date. This statement is particularly useful if you want to do a detailed analysis of a particular fund.

- The *statement of changes in net assets* shows all the factors that increased or decreased the fund's net assets from the year before.

Auditor:
*Accountant
who verifies
a fund
company's
financial
statements.*

- While a *statement of portfolio transactions* is not ordinarily included in the financial statements, you can ask for a copy at any time. It will be sent to you at no charge.

Except for the statement of investment portfolio, these statements are rarely of much use. As well, key information is often summarized for you elsewhere in the annual or semi-annual report, and also in other sources such as newspapers.

**Coupon
rate:**
*The rate of
interest a
bond pays,
usually fixed
and paid in
equal
installments
twice a year.*

The annual information form

Although the simplified prospectus and the financial statements must be in your hands as you make your decision, you must simply be told that you can also have the annual information form. This document is very similar to the simplified prospectus but more detailed, particularly on the risks, distribution and tax information. The simplified prospectus for one popular Canadian equity growth fund is 16 pages, while the annual information form is more than double that — 36 pages.

Exceptions to the simplified prospectus system

Some mutual funds cannot use the simplified prospectus system. These include real estate and commodity funds. Instead, these funds must issue a lengthy traditional prospectus. A traditional prospectus has three parts: A description of the fund and the securities it holds, details of the fund's operations and recent and historical financial statements. The fund must follow the same laws and deadlines as with a simplified prospectus and your rights are the same.

Check your account statement

Your personal account statements will be sent to you at the end of each quarter or at the end of any month in which there has been activity in your account. These statements will detail your holdings and their value, as well as any activity that has taken place.

You might also find a breakdown of your mutual fund investments by asset class — equity, fixed-income or cash — as a percentage of your portfolio. This can help you monitor the mix of investments in your portfolio. If your account is an RRSP account, then the amount of foreign content in your portfolio is also shown.

Always read your account statements for

Commodity fund:
A high-risk fund that trades futures contracts on oil, grain and currencies.

possible errors and diligently file them away for future reference. If you notice an error on your statement, call your advisor or the fund company immediately and make notes of your conversation, including the date and time of the call, and the names of the people you spoke to. Follow up in writing if you feel it's necessary.

Where to buy mutual funds

With so many mutual funds available, and so many different outlets selling funds, the issue of where to buy mutual funds might seem a tad trite. But it's one of the most important considerations for any investor. Which fund seller you choose to work with will dictate the variety of funds at your disposal, the commissions you will pay, and the level of advice you can expect.

No one type of fund selling company is clearly better than the other. Your choice should be determined by your own needs. If you're making your own fund selections, then commission schedules and fund choices will be important to you. If your needs are complex and your knowledge limited, then you'll want to get and pay for expert advice.

Fortunately, there's a wide range of fund sellers in Canada, each catering to a different clientele and offering different kinds of service.

• Financial institutions, such as banks, trust companies and life insurance companies usually sell their own mutual funds and provide some advice to their clients without charging commission.

- Full-service brokerage firms or investment dealers provide advice on hundreds of different funds as well as other investments like stocks and bonds for a commission or fee.

- Discount brokerage firms provide access to hundreds of different funds and other investments at very low cost, but generally don't advise clients what funds to buy.

- Mutual fund dealers, sometimes called financial planning firms, provide advice on a wide range of funds for a commission or fee.

- Direct sellers are fund companies that sell their funds direct to the public through their own offices or agency sales forces.

- Union and trade or professional associations, such as the Canadian Dental Association, sell funds to their members and their families.

Getting wide choice

When shopping for mutual funds, remember that the variety of funds available to you will hinge on the type of dealer you choose. Typically, financial institutions like banks and direct sellers only sell their own funds. Brokerage firms and mutual fund dealers sell funds from many different fund companies, including bank funds. Using one of these firms gives you many more options to choose from.

Mutual fund dealer: *A firm that sells mostly mutual funds from many companies and whose salespeople often call themselves financial planners.*

Investment dealer: *A firm that sells a large variety of mutual funds, stocks, bonds and other products and whose salespeople are called investment advisors (IAs).*

Salary vs. commission

Another key difference between fund distributors is how their salespeople are compensated. In general, banks and some direct sellers pay salaries with a portion based on commission, while sales staff at brokerages, fund dealers and the remaining direct sellers work almost exclusively on commission.

The choice of working with a commissioned or salaried advisor is a personal one. It's often overlooked that commissioned salespeople have more incentive to serve you well to ensure repeat business. Salaried advisors rely more on their employers paying them a salary than on your continued satisfaction, which can mean the employer's interests will be put first. On the other hand, commissioned sales people might be inclined to put their own self-interest ahead of yours, while the salaried advisor has less to gain personally by selling you one fund over another. As we said, neither is clearly better than the other, so it's best to select an advisor based on critieria such as their experience, knowledge, and your comfort level with them.

How fund salespeople are regulated

The boom in mutual funds in Canada has raised some concerns about how well investors are protected from dubious sales practices. In many respects, the industry has grown faster than the regulations that govern it. Nonetheless, significant strides have been made to improve industry standards.

The ultimate responsibility for protecting consumers when it comes to investments lies with the provincial government bodies called securities administrators or commissions. However, most brokerages — distinct from banks, insurance and mutual fund dealers — are subject to a second level of governance by Self-Regulatory Organizations (SROs). The SROs include the Investment Dealers Association of Canada (IDA) and the four major stock exchanges in Montreal, Toronto, Alberta and Vancouver. In general, the standards required by the SROs often exceed the standards the provinces set.

SRO:
Industry body that regulates its members under the watchful eye of the provincial governments.

Different levels of oversight

In other words, all advisors who sell mutual funds are not regulated in the same way. Some are subject to two levels of regulation while others are subject to one. Knowing this when you deal with an advisor will help you understand the standards he or she must comply with. Moves are currently afoot to introduce a new SRO for all mutual fund dealers led by the IDA and the Investment Funds Institute of Canada (IFIC), the fund industry's trade association. This organization, called the Mutual Fund Dealers Association, is supposed to raise minimum standards for everyone who sells mutual funds.

So, in the meantime, how do you identify advisors who are subject to increased levels of oversight? A simple rule of thumb is to find out if the advisor's firm is covered by the Canadian Investor Protection Fund (CIPF). CIPF protects you

How your advisor is licensed

Fund managers, distributors and their salespeople must be registered with the securities commission in every province in which they work or sell. Not only must this registration be kept up-to-date, regulators must be told within five business days of changes that could affect the registration status.

For salespeople this includes changes in their personal circumstances such as a change of address or employer, personal bankruptcy, or a change in employment. If a mutual fund salesperson leaves his or her employer, most commissions will suspend the license until a new employer confirms that the person has been hired.

Salespeople must also have passed either the Canadian Securities Course™ offered by the Canadian Securities Institute or courses offered by the Investment Funds Institute of Canada and the Institute of Canadian Bankers.

against loss due to the financial failure of any firm in the SRO system. CIPF covers losses up to $500,000 for securities and cash balances. Coverage for cash is limited to $60,000. Mutual funds are included in the definition of securities. CIPF does not cover market losses. Only firms governed by the SROs can be members of the CIPF. All members of the CIPF have to indicate their membership in all advertisements, marketing brochures and in their offices, so it shouldn't be hard to find out if your firm is a member.

Of course, while membership in the CIPF and regulation by an SRO offers you increased protection from dubious practices, it's not foolproof. To help you spot potential problems early, you need to know what standards your advisor is expected to meet.

Protection

How your advisor should behave

All mutual fund sellers must abide by the same basic rule of every advisor-client relationship — *know your client*. This rule, also known as the suitability rule, tries to ensure that your advisor only recommends funds

You can expect certain standards of advice and service.

to you that fit your objectives, risk tolerance and time horizons.

In addition, your advisor must also live up to the requirements of a national sales practices rule. The focus of the so-called Mutual Fund Sales Practices Rule is to protect you from conflicts of interest and potential abuse. Some of the issues covered in the new code include:

Unacceptable sales practices

There are a number of things that sales people might be tempted to do — such as distorting the performance of a fund — that are unacceptable to regulators. Engaging in these and any other kind of unethical behavior could cause a salesperson to be banned from the industry.

The Investment Funds Institute ethical guidelines

The industry has a code of practice to guide the behavior of mutual funds salespeople. While these are only guidelines, they reflect the very minimum standards you should expect wherever you choose to buy mutual funds:

- Benefits of other investments, such as individual stocks and bonds, are not to be disparaged.

- The "know your client" rule must be strictly followed. Your advisor must know enough about your age, occupation and marital status as well as your investment and financial goals to make sure an investment is suitable for you. When opening an ongoing purchase plan, you will also be asked for further details, such as the age of your dependants. If you refuse to give any of this information you will probably be asked to sign a waiver.

- Information is to be held in the strictest confidence and used only to judge the suitability of investments.

- Your advisor should not recommend a fund if he or she does not firmly believe that it fits your objectives, financial situation and needs.

- An advisor should not encourage you to borrow excessively to invest in mutual funds. Borrowing can be a sound strategy, but both your advisor and you should be careful.

- An advisor should not recommend replacing existing investments unless your interests will be better met and all costs and implications are made clear to you.

- Sales material given to you, such as brochures, advertisements, videos, cassettes, or newsletters, must clearly show the name of the author, the offering company or the fund.

Backdating purchase orders

When you place an order for mutual funds, you don't know what price you are paying because it will be based on the NAVPS at the end of the next valuation day. It's illegal for your advisor to backdate an order and pretend to have bought the funds on an earlier date.

Valuation date: *The day on which a fund's value is calculated to arrive at the price per unit, usually done daily.*

Guaranteed repurchase or refund

Your advisor cannot offer to buy your fund back from you in an effort to protect you from losing money. Of course, you always have the right to redeem you fund units at any time.

Advertising

Advisors cannot advertise the fact that they are registered with a securities authority. This rule is meant to avoid the appearance that the regulators endorse the advisor.

Promising a future price

Salespeople cannot make promises that a fund will reach a particular price in the future. This is like promising that you will earn a certain return, which is impossible to predict in a mutual fund.

Death, Taxes
and Mutual
Fund Fees

Fund costs vary widely, but they all have one thing in common – they're inescapable.

Fund managers have to earn a living, too

Used to be that two things in life were certain — death and taxes. Nowadays you could add a third certainty to the mix — death, taxes and *mutual fund fees*. That's because no matter how you cut it, you are going to have to pay for the professional management, diversification and ready access to your cash that you get through mutual funds.

While it's probably unfair to dump mutual fund fees in with taxes and mortality, the point must be made that there is no such thing as a free fund. Many people who invest in no-load funds believe they're avoiding fees. The truth, however, is that every mutual fund investor pays fees, whether they know it or not. This is because every fund company takes money out of the fund to pay expenses. Because you won't see this reflected on your account statement, many people aren't aware they're paying the fund's operational costs.

Professional management has a price
Before you get the wrong impression about the mutual fund industry's fee structure, it's important to put the fees into perspective. Remember all those benefits of mutual funds we listed in the first chapter of this book? Well, a raft of advantages that long doesn't come without a price.

The price reflects the fact that you are paying a professional money manager to decide for you what investments to buy and sell. This kind of expertise would generally be out of reach for many people if not for mutual funds. If you have $1,000 available to invest, then you might pay $20 in management fees for a year of professional money management. That's good value for the services of a highly trained and experienced money manager.

Of course, you wouldn't consider it good value if the fund manager's decisions cause your investment to drop in value. That's one of the reasons mutual fund fees are a perennial topic of hot debate – you pay them regardless of how well or poorly the fund performs. Seeing your $1,000

investment drop in value to $900 and then having salt rubbed in your wounds with a $20 management fee is never going to be popular with the paying public.

However, in a more positive scenario where your fund manager's stock picking prowess grows your investment by 20% or more, then that $20 fee does seem like good value. In fact, the controversy over mutual fund fees is not so much that they exist, but the fact that few people fully understand them. The confusion is mostly a result of there being several types of fees. They vary depending on where you buy a fund, the type of fund you buy, how long you own the fund plus a host of other factors.

Two main costs you pay

In simple terms, though, you face two main costs when you buy a mutual fund. These are:

- Sales fees that you might pay either when you buy or when you sell fund units. In mutual fund industry jargon, sales fees or commissions are called loads. You have three main types to choose between. Front-end loads are charged when you buy a fund, back-end loads when you sell and no-load funds do not charge sales fees. If you buy a mutual fund with a sales fee, then most fund companies will give you a choice between paying either a front-end load, or a back-end load. However, a few funds charge both front and back-end loads. These should be avoided unless there is a compelling reason to do otherwise.

- Ongoing management and administration fees that you pay for as long as you own a fund, but which aren't billed to you directly. You will find information about these fees in a fund's prospectus, usually in a summary table near the front.

Front-end loads

Front-end load:
A fee you pay when you buy a fund; based on the amount invested.

You pay this commission when you buy the fund. The fee is a percentage of the money you are investing. The percentage typically ranges from around 2% to 7%. With a front-end load, part of your money goes into the sales commission, so not all of your cash is invested. This impacts on the return your money will earn.

Consider an example using a 5% front-end load. On a $1,000 investment, $50 goes to the commission and $950 will actually end up being invested. In actuality, your front-end load percentage is higher than you think. Since you are only investing $950, that $50 commission you paid works out to 5.26% of your investment.

Now let's say the fund in which you invest earns a return of 10%, which means your $950 grows to $1,045. Not a bad gain, but if you use your original $1,000 as your starting value, then you've only earned a 4.5% return. In other words, the front-end load has actually denied you the opportunity to get an extra 5.5% return on your money. In dollar terms, the $50 front-end load has actually cost you $55.

You invest $1,000 in a 5% front-end load fund that earns a 10% return. But what's your actual return on your original investment?

You invest:	$1,000
Advisor takes:	$50
Actual investment:	$950
After 10% return:	$1,045
Your actual return:	4.5%

Lower ongoing fees

Front-end load funds often charge lower ongoing management fees than other types of funds. If you're investing for a long period, you may pay more in up-front commission, but less over time compared to the generally higher management costs of back-end load and some no-load funds. The time needed to make the front-end load more economical depends largely on how much commission you pay up-front, and how big the difference between the two management fees is. When the difference in management fees is 0.25%, a front-end load of 5% becomes more economical than a back-end or no-load fund after about 12 years. The less you pay in commission up-front, and the bigger the difference between the management fees, the quicker the front-end load option becomes more economical.

Negotiating a lower charge

You can negotiate with your advisor to lower the front-end commission, especially if you're investing a large sum. As well, a number of discount brokerages have started to waive the commission on front-end load funds, essentially making them no-load funds.

If you are investing for a period of three years or less, then a front-end load can be cheaper than back-end loads, which charge higher commissions for short-term investment. This is one reason why people who trade funds relatively often choose front-end or no-load funds.

Back-end loads

Also known as deferred sales charges (DSCs), back-end loads have become more popular in recent years because Canadians have resisted paying an up-front charge. However, in their haste to avoid the up-front fee, some people might be overlooking a couple key drawbacks.

Back-end loads are designed for longer-term investment and penalize people who withdraw their money after just a year or two. The earlier you withdraw your money, the higher the commission you pay. Typically, the commission starts at around 6% in year one and gradually declines to nil in years six to eight. The fee structure is non-negotiable.

Since one of the key lessons of this book is that most mutual funds are for longer-term investment, you might think the back-end load is the option to go for. After all, it rewards you for keeping your money invested longer. But that might not be altogether true.

Deferred sales charge (DSC): *A percentage fee you pay when you sell a fund. Higher for shorter investment periods and based on original or withdrawal value.*

Cost countdown

Money withdrawn	% commission
Year 1	6
Year 2	5.5
Year 3	5
Year 4	4.5
Year 5	4
Year 6	3
Year 7	nil

Typical declining back-end load schedule.

Moral Hazard: *The catch-22 when you want to sell a back-end load fund but are put off by the high sales fee.*

Beware of catch-22

A catch with back-end loads is that they typically carry higher ongoing management expenses than similar front-end load funds. That means you are paying the fund company more to manage the fund than you would if you'd opted for the up-front fee. And since the back-end load structure penalizes those who cash out early, more people are encouraged to leave their money in the fund for longer. This means the fund company gets to charge the higher management fee and expenses on a larger base of "captive" investors.

Another drawback is what's sometimes called *moral hazard* – the risk or dilemma that arises when you invest in a back-end load fund and then want to move out because it fails to live up to your expectations. If this happens in the first year or two, you will have to pay the higher commission. You may decide to stay in the fund to avoid the high

Small detail, big difference

Two investors contribute $10,000 each to back-end load funds that earn 10% per year for three years. Both have to pay 4.5% commission when they cash out, but investor A's load is calculated on the amount invested, while investor B's is based on the current value. Here's what each has left after commission:

	Investor A	Investor B
Invested:	$10,000.00	$10,000.00
After 3 yrs:	$13,310.00	$13,310.00
Load:	4.5% of $10,000.00 = $450.00	4.5% of $13,310.00 = $598.50
Total after load:	$12,860.00	$12,711.50
Annual compound average return	9.53%	9.04%

Investor A earns almost half a per cent more over three years because of the difference in how the back-end load is calculated.

commission, even though you don't like the fund. In most cases, it will be best to sell a fund that no longer matches your objectives. Of course, if you're already disgruntled with the fund, because it lost money, then that 6% sales charge is really going to get you steamed. You will be especially upset if the commission is based on the amount you originally invested and not on the lower amount your investment is worth at withdrawal.

That's right, the back-end load can be calculated on either how much you invested or how much you take out. Most fund companies charge you on the original amount invested. But if it's based on the cash-out value, you could face a higher cost, assuming the value of your investment has grown (see chart opposite).

All of this, however, might be offset by two key advantages of back-end load funds. First is a feature that lets you withdraw 10% of your money per year without paying the load. In effect, this is a no-load way to invest in back-end load funds.

The second advantage over front-end load funds is that all your money goes to work for you inside the fund. The advantage of this can be significant over longer periods, since more of your money is working for you. If your intention is to hold the fund for six or more years and the fund has lower than average management expenses, then the back-end load may be to your advantage.

Back-end rebates are an advantage

Back-end loads can also be more attractive if your fund seller gives you part of the typical 5% commission it gets from the fund company when your money goes in. Discount brokerages in particular offer rebates — typically 2% to 3% of the amount you invest. This is like getting an instant return on your investment. The rebate is paid in extra fund units rather than cash. If you get a rebate on units held outside a registered plan such as your RRSP, the rebate's value will be included in your income. But you can file an

Adjusted cost base: *Your initial cost for fund units plus reinvested distributions and any additional purchases; used to determine your capital gain or loss.*

election under the Income Tax Act to stop this amount from being included in your income. If the election is filed, the rebate amount will reduce the adjusted cost base of the fund units. So the rebate ends up being taxed once those fund units are sold. There's no special form to file. Just remember to add a statement to your tax return saying you are making the election under section 53 (2.1) of the Act. If you get the commission rebate on mutual funds bought inside your RRSP or RRIF, you don't need to worry about that amount being included in your income. The rebate isn't considered to be a contribution to your plan. So it doesn't reduce your RRSP contribution room.

When choosing a back-end load, you should weigh the lack of short-term flexibility and the generally higher management expenses against the benefits of all your money, plus any rebates, going to work for you immediately.

No-load funds

No load:
A fund that has no sales fees but which still charges management expenses.

You can avoid a sales charge altogether if you buy a no-load fund. Most banks, trusts and a few independent companies sell no-load funds. They don't charge loads because they generally have their own networks of salaried salespeople and don't have to rely on third-party firms to sell their funds. Load fund companies, on the other hand, rely heavily on brokerage firms and mutual fund dealers to sell their funds. The sales fees are how the load fund companies compensate the dealers for selling their funds.

One potential disadvantage of no-load funds is the very fact that they don't pay commissions. The argument goes that since the person most often selling a no-load fund gets paid a salary, they have less incentive to make you happy.

Commission-based salespeople, however, can only earn a sustained living if their clients feel they are getting value for the sales fee they are paying. This extra value, it's argued, comes in the form of better recommendations. Commissioned salespeople such as investment advisors at brokerage firms typically offer you access to a wider array of funds than salaried fund sellers who have tended in the past to sell only their employer's funds.

However, there's a counter argument to the one just detailed. It says that you may get as good advice from a salaried salesperson as from a commission-based one. The only downfall of the salaried advisor might be that they generally only offer their employer's proprietary funds. However, most banks today offer a wide range of mutual funds to suit just about any investment objective.

Salaried advisor: *A fund seller, typically at a bank, who earns a salary rather than commission.*

Watch for ongoing fees

Another frequently cited drawback is that management fees on a no-load fund will be higher than on a load fund. In some cases this is true, although management expenses between no-load funds and load funds are much the same on average. In fact, some of the newer no-load funds have lower

**Manage-
ment fee:**
*Fee paid to
fund
manager for
selecting
investments
and
managing
the
portfolio,
usually a
percentage
based on
the total
value of the
fund.*

**Operational
expenses:**
*All costs
other than
the
manage-
ment fee
incurred in
running the
fund.*

management expense structures than many front-end
load funds, which traditionally have had the lowest
management expenses.

The obvious benefits of the no-load structure are
that you have no sales fees to worry about, and all your
money goes to work in the fund.

With all their pros and cons, you might well be
wondering which load option then is the best. The
answer is that sales fees alone don't give you the full
picture of the costs of investing in a particular fund.
You also have to tally in the ongoing management
expenses. Only then will you have a true reading on
the costs of a particular fund.

Management fees and expenses

All mutual funds have management and operational or
administrative costs that you pay indirectly. Many
people don't realize they are paying these fees because
they are deducted from the fund before it publishes its
returns. The expenses are charged to your investments
regardless of whether the fund makes you money or not.

A management fee is paid to the mutual fund
management company for its portfolio management
expertise. This fee may vary depending on which load
you choose. A front-end load fund might have a lower
management fee than a back-end load or a no-load
fund. Some fund companies offer negotiable
management fees, with the percentage you pay
declining as the amount you invest in a fund or family
of funds increases. Others have management fee
structures that reward the fund manager for better than
average performance.

Operational and administrative expenses include legal and auditing costs, regulatory filing fees, accounting, marketing, brokerage commissions and on-going service payments to your advisor.

Bill break-out

Fees and expenses you pay indirectly

- Portfolio manager's fee
- Legal and auditing costs
- Taxes
- Brokerage commissions
- Salaries
- Customer service
- Printing of prospectuses
- Advertising
- Trailer fees

Trailer fees go to your advisor

The on-going payments your advisor might get are called service or trailer fees. They are paid as long as your money stays in the fund. The fee varies from about 0.25% to 1% per year of the money you have in the fund. Much controversy has surrounded trailer fees in recent years mostly because they raise the possibility for conflict of interest.

Trailer fee:
Controversial fee fund company pays to fund sellers for as long as clients' money remains in fund. Also called a "service fee."

Since trailers differ from fund to fund and between fund companies, there is a financial incentive for an advisor to sell the fund that pays the higher trailer fee. There is also an incentive to keep clients in mutual funds rather than move their money into other products such as GICs or Canada Savings Bonds, which might serve the client better.

The industry's argument is that trailers are meant to pay advisors for the ongoing services they give you, such as answering questions about your account. It's also argued that the trailer fee amount is based on the value of the assets in the fund, so it's in your advisor's interests to help you choose your funds wisely. As assets grow, so does the advisor's trailer fee. If you want to know what trailer fee your advisor stands to earn on particular funds, then you can ask your advisor outright or look up the fee schedule in the fund's simplified prospectus. If your advisor is recommending one particular fund, ask what would be his or her second and third choice of funds so that you can compare them. By checking the trailer fees of all three funds in the prospectus, you can assess if there is any incentive for your advisor to recommend one fund over the others.

The management expense ratio (MER)

The management expense ratio (MER) is a useful tool to compare the ongoing costs of investing in different funds. It tells you roughly how much you are paying in management fees and expenses each year.

The MER takes all but a few of the different expenses (brokerage costs aren't included) and expresses them as a percentage of the fund's total value. If the fund is worth $1 billion and the management fee and operational expenses amount to $25 million, then the fund will have a 2.5% MER. If your investment in the same fund is worth $10,000 then you will have paid $250 in management fees and expenses in the year.

Although MERs might appear to be small percentages, they have an impact on a fund's performance and can add up over the long term. A

Median MERs by fund type

Fund Type	Median	Range
Asia/Pacific Rim equity	2.78	1.25 - 3.81
Asia ex-Japan equity	2.88	2.21 - 8.98
Canadian tactical asset allocation	2.27	0.52 - 3.48
Canadian balanced	2.1	0.05 - 3.48
Canadian bond	1.48	0.16 - 2.92
Canadian dividend income	1.7	1.09 - 2.7
Canadian equity	2.3	0.09 - 3.52
Canadian high income balanced	1.68	1.16 - 3.51
Canadian large-cap equity	2.19	0.5 - 2.88
Canadian money market	0.78	0.05 - 1.71
Canadian mortgage	1.57	0.75 - 2.3
Canadian short-term bond	1.3	0.7 - 2.26
Canadian small and mid-cap equity	2.4	1. - 3.46
Country specific	1.82	1.6 - 3.74
Emerging markets equity	2.83	0.2 - 4.84
European equity	2.47	0.9 - 3.03
Foreign bond	2.02	0.45 - 6.25
Foreign money market	1.1	0.52 - 2.69
Global balanced and asset allocation	2.46	0.21 - 3.15
Global equity	2.5	0.32 - 3.57
Natural resources	2.44	2 - 4.01
Precious metals	2.47	2.07 - 7.86
Science and technology	2.56	1.05 - 3.3
International equity	2	0.2 - 2.98
Japanese equity	2.46	0.9 - 3.07
Labor-sponsored venture capital	4.7	1.6 - 12.09
Latin American equity	3.48	2.34 - 8.49
North American equity	2.3	1.18 - 3.5
Specialty or miscellaneous	2.49	1 - 5.21
U.S. equity	2.03	0.05 - 3.56
U.S. small and mid-cap equity	2.5	0.41 - 2.99
Real estate	2.5	0.43 - 2.73
Unclassified	3.34	3.34 - 3.34

Source: BellCharts Inc. at Dec. 31, 1998

MER debate

MERs — which affect your return from a mutual fund — have been going up, instead of down. Although Canadians are pouring billions of dollars into mutual funds, this has not created greater economies of scale. Or, if it has, Canadian investors have not felt it in their own pockets.

The fund industry has blamed the jump in MERs on the cost of switching from front-end loads to deferred commissions and trailer fees — at the demand of investors. But Canadian MERs have been higher than in the U.S., and many other countries, for decades.

Several reasons have been given for this: U.S. funds are larger, allowing greater economies of scale, with several funds managing assets larger than the entire Canadian market; distribution costs are not included in U.S. funds; and, Canadian mutual funds tend to invest in more foreign securities, which is expensive.

Some industry watchers are not convinced. They say Canadian fund companies are just charging what the market will bear and will continue doing so until investors ask for a better deal.

MER of 3% rather than 2% on a fund which generates a 12% annual return means you end up with a return of about 8.6% instead of 9.7%. The difference in return may seem minor, but it adds up over time. A $20,000 investment that earns 9.7% a year for 20 years would grow to $127,398 — compared to $104,142 at 8.6%. That's a $23,256 difference — not small by most people's standards.

Why MERs vary between funds

MERs reflect many things, including the type of asset the fund invests in, and the fund's objectives. Stock investing tends to be a more labor-intensive and costly activity than fixed-income investing. Costs will vary even between different types of equity funds. Those that invest in overseas markets, smaller companies or select industries are typically more expensive to run than broadly invested Canadian equity funds. This is because these special equity funds demand more research and analysis, plus higher fees for trading internationally.

Money market funds, fixed-income funds and index funds tend to have the lowest MERs. For these, the impact of management fees and expenses is greater. Index funds hold set baskets of stocks or bonds and therefore do little trading so costs are lower. There tends to be a strong link between low MERs and top performance in these three fund categories. This is because managers of these funds have less scope to add value by picking investments and fewer opportunities to outperform their peers. So high costs will hurt their performance.

A fund's MER will be lower, even zero, if it does not charge its fees and expenses to the fund itself but to you directly. Be aware that some fund companies do this. MERs are also lower on funds available only to pension plan managers and wealthy investors

Portfolio fund:
A fund that invests in other mutual funds rather than individual investments, resulting in higher underlying management expenses.

What to look out for

An occasional problem is that companies package their expenses differently. Some companies only report their management fee, not their MER. Some "portfolio" funds, which invest in other mutual funds, do not publish the management cost to you for the underlying funds.

When comparing MERs, make sure you are comparing apples to apples. You can find the MERs for individual funds, and averages for fund types, listed in newspapers like The Globe and Mail's Report on Mutual Funds, published the third Thursday of the month. The Financial Post section of the National Post also publishes a monthly mutual fund report on the second Saturday of the month.

Other fees

Aside from charges for selling, redeeming and managing your mutual funds, fund companies may charge for various other services.

Set-up fees

Some no-load fund companies levy a one-time set-up or administration fee of about $50.

Early redemption fee

Some funds will charge a fee if you redeem your units within 90 days of purchase. The fee is usually assessed at 2% of your investment. Even no-load companies make use of this charge to discourage you from short-term trading and to cover the administrative costs of your buy and sell transactions.

Transfer or switching fees

You may choose to switch from one fund to another within the same family for various reasons. Perhaps a change in objective — yours or the fund's — has made the fund you're holding unsuitable. Or maybe after much thought, you've decided to move to another type of fund. The switching or transfer fee is charged at the financial advisor or mutual fund dealer's discretion. Most fund companies let advisors charge you as much as 2% of your investment when you switch. Often fund sellers waive this fee, although what you pay depends on your relationship with your advisor. Direct sellers and no-load companies tend to waive transfer fees.

RRSP trustee fees

If you hold your mutual funds inside a Registered Retirement Savings Plan (RRSP), Registered Retire-ment Income Fund (RRIF) or a Registered Education Savings Plan (RESP), you might be charged an annual trustee fee of between $25 and $75. These fees may be negotiable, or might be waived, particularly if you are making or maintaining a sizeable investment.

A final word on fees

Make sure your comparisons of MERs and other fees are of funds in the same category. While you should consider the impact that fees will have on your investment returns, you shouldn't let them dictate your final investment decision. What a fund is going to cost you should be just one of the things you look at. Other things to consider are your investment objectives, your tolerance for risk and the fund's long-term record of stable returns. That having been said, if two funds seem to offer equal potential to meet your objectives, then the cheaper of the two will be the logical choice.

Navigating
The Fund
Universe

The funds you need to achieve your investment objectives are somewhere out there. Here's a guide to help you find them.

In Canada today there are almost 2,000 mutual funds for you to choose from. That's both a good and a bad thing. While you have the benefit of a lot more choice, you also have the headache of sorting through the maze of mutual fund options. In fact, even the fund industry itself has had trouble trying to put categories around the plethora of available fund alternatives. So it's not hard to see why so many new mutual fund investors have had a ton of trouble trying to find funds that are suitable for them.

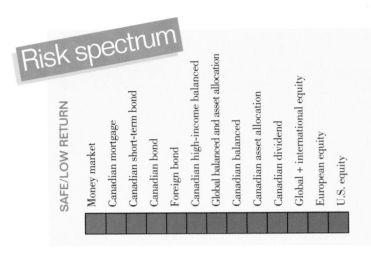

Fortunately, the industry appears to have found a way to segment the fund universe into about 33 broad categories. This is a far cry from the days when funds in Canada were commonly divided between those that were or weren't RRSP-eligible. Having these categories makes it easier for you to find the funds that might match your personal objectives. It also lets you better compare the performance of similar funds.

These new categories used to describe funds are based on the kinds of investments, or mix of investments, that the funds hold. These fund groups can then be broken down by the region of the world or industry in which they invest, the maturity or size of the companies held, or the term-to-maturity of bonds in the portfolio. However, just because a fund is grouped in a particular category doesn't mean it actually has the same kind of investments as others in its group. The best way to tell what's in a fund is to check the portfolio. You

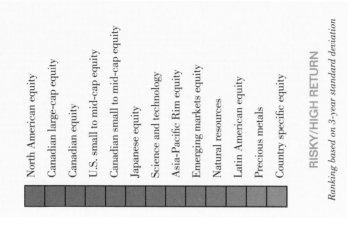

North American equity | Canadian large-cap equity | Canadian equity | U.S. small to mid-cap equity | Canadian small to mid-cap equity | Japanese equity | Science and technology | Asia-Pacific Rim equity | Emerging markets equity | Natural resources | Latin American equity | Precious metals | Country specific equity

RISKY/HIGH RETURN

Ranking based on 3-year standard deviation

can find this information in the fund's statement of portfolio holdings.

Grouping funds by their risk-return profile

The approach of grouping funds by their risk-return profile is not something you will commonly see used in mutual fund prospectuses or newspapers. However, it is used in this book because it will make your understanding of the different fund categories easier. It will also let you quickly identify the fund groups most likely to be of interest to you.

We will start with the safest funds and gradually discuss each fund type through to the riskiest types. To get a snapshot of all the fund types arranged from safest to riskiest, look at the risk-return spectrum. The safest fund type — money market funds — sits on the left of the spectrum. These funds also offer the lowest potential return. On the right of the spectrum are country specific equity funds, a category that offers the highest return potential but also the biggest risk of loss.

Of course, in reality the safest funds don't always have the lowest returns, nor do country-specific funds have the highest. Still, the spectrum will give you a general idea of the risk and return potential of each fund type. As we will see in a later chapter, your goal must be to find funds that fit your objectives and which offer the highest potential return with the least amount of risk. Also remember that risk-return profiles can change over time. As well, some fund types have been excluded from our spectrum because of inadequate or misleading data.

Money market: *Where securites with terms of less than one year are bought and sold.*

Money market funds

As the safest fund type, money market funds are often considered a good substitute for savings accounts, GICs and other cash and cash equivalent assets. Their objective is to safeguard your money and provide you with low, but steady income. This is why money market funds are often recommended for the cash portion — usually 5% to 10% — of a balanced portfolio. They are also ideal when you are investing for a short-term goal and don't want to risk your principal.

Advisors often recommend money market funds to clients who are uncertain of where they want to invest their money. This often happens in the rush near the end of February when Canadians traditionally make last-minute contributions to their RRSPs. Instead of making a rash decision, the idea is to get the money invested in a safe vehicle, from which it can later be moved when you've made up your mind.

An extension of this theme is the concept of using money market funds to "park" your money when the markets are highly volatile, particularly if there are fears of rising inflation. Higher inflation, which in turn can lead to higher general interest rates, can result in lower stock and bond prices. The effect is greatest on longer-term investments and least on short-term money market securities. Shifting your money to cash investments can shield you from the short-term impact of inflation. However, this strategy involves trying to time the market, something that is extremely difficult to do with success and therefore unsuitable for most investors.

Two types of money market funds
There are two main types of money market funds — U.S. and Canadian. Typically, Canadian money market funds hold more than 90% of their money in short-term Canadian investments. The remainder is made up of short-term investments from the U.S., Japan or Europe.

U.S. money market funds hold money market instruments of American issuers or Canadian securities denominated in U.S. dollars, or both. When you buy a money market fund denominated

Market timing:
Trying to predict which investment class will earn the highest returns over a defined period.

Park:
Leave money in a safe place for a short time.

Rating agency:
Firm that ranks the likelihood that an issuer won't be able to repay debts.

in U.S. dollars, you will gain if the Canadian dollar weakens against the American currency. The risk, of course, is if the Canadian dollar strengthens against the U.S. dollar, which will reduce your return.

Both Canadian and U.S. funds hold high quality short-term debt investments such as government treasury bills (T-bills), commercial paper and government bonds maturing in less than one year. Some money market funds will hold a mix of all of these, while others will confine themselves to a single investment type, such as T-bills or commercial paper. Fund managers will sometimes restrict themselves to investing in instruments awarded the highest rankings by independent debt rating agencies.

What typical money market funds hold

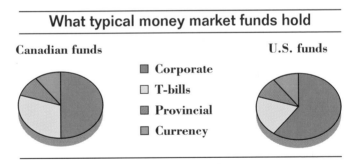

Canadian funds   U.S. funds

■ Corporate
□ T-bills
■ Provincial
■ Currency

There is generally little to choose between money market funds since returns are quite similar. Look closely at a money market fund's fee structure. If you're investing for a short-term goal, you don't want to be hit with a high back-end load when you cash out. While most funds charge MERs in the 1% range, some may charge as much as 2.5% or more. A high MER can hurt your return, particularly when interest rates on short-term investments are low.

Money market funds do not realize any growth because net asset value per share is usually kept at $10 and all income is distributed to you. These distributions can be paid in cash or you can use them to buy more shares of the fund. The usual minimum initial investment is between $500 and $1,000, though some require as much as $25,000.

Fixed-income funds

Most people should have at least part of their portfolio allocated to fixed-income assets. They can add stability to your portfolio and over the long-term will generally move in opposite directions to stock funds. When stock funds are doing badly, their poor performance can be offset by fixed-income funds' stability. As you will see, however, there is no guarantee that you won't lose money investing in fixed-income funds.

Fixed-income funds' performance is directly tied to the trend in interest rates. As interest rates rise, a fixed-income fund's unit value falls. As rates fall, your units will increase in value. The depth of the rise and fall in unit value depends on many factors. A key factor is the average term-to-maturity of the fund's investments. This is the number of years before the securities in the fund can be cashed for their face value. The longer the average term-to-maturity, the greater will be the

Face value:
A bond's denomination, the lump sum you get back when it matures.

Bond quality:
The credit rating of the bond issuer affects the bond's quality.

impact when interest rates change. Other factors affecting the magnitude of a fund's reaction to rate changes is the quality and coupon size of the securities in the fund. Lower average coupons and lower average quality — say a lot of corporate bonds — make a bond fund more volatile.

One reason you would choose fixed-income funds is for their steady income. Most of these funds invest in securities that pay regular amounts of interest. These interest payments are typically passed on to you, either monthly, quarterly or annually. Check the fund's prospectus to see how frequently interest payments are made. You should also keep in mind that the interest income from these funds is taxed at your full tax rate. This makes fixed-income funds ideal for holding inside a tax-sheltered RRSP.

While most fixed-income funds focus on earning income, some also invest for capital gains. One strategy for these managers is to buy fixed-income securities before interest rates fall, after which they can usually sell at a profit. Another strategy is to buy cheap bonds of issuers whose credit ratings have deteriorated or who are in default. If the issuer recovers, the bonds will regain value and the manager can sell at a profit.

Canadian mortgage funds
Often overlooked, these funds can offer a good trade-off between risk and return. While returns

What typical mortgage funds hold

☐ **Mortgage-backed securities**

☐ **Cash**

☐ **Canadian bonds**

are usually modest, their NAVPS fluctuates less than for other fixed-income funds, making them less risky. This is why some people use mortgage funds as alternatives to money market funds or term deposits.

Mortgage funds, most of which are RRSP eligible, aim for safety of principal and regular income, paid either monthly, quarterly or annually. Their portfolios consist of Canadian industrial, commercial and/or residential mortgages and mortgage-backed securities. Mortgage funds usually have average terms to maturity of less than five years, making them less risky than funds with longer terms to maturity.

You should also be aware that not all mortgage funds are created equal. Most are pure mortgage funds, while a handful hold a mix of mortgages and bonds of various maturities, making them a little more volatile. This underscores the importance of analyzing the fund's portfolio before you invest.

One disadvantage of mortgage funds is that they typically have higher average MERs than money market and some bond funds.

Mortgage-backed security:
A unit of a pool of insured home mortgages that pays interest and part of principal.

Canadian short-term bond funds

With average terms to maturity of less than five years and more than one year, short-term bond funds invest in short-term Canadian government and corporate bonds and mortgage-backed securities. Because of the shorter term-to-maturity, these funds are less volatile than regular Canadian bond funds.

What typical short-term bond funds hold

■ **Short-term government bonds**
□ **Short-term corporate bonds**
■ **Mortgage-backed securities**
□ **Cash**

In fact, these funds are often sold as an alternative to GICs. They are less exposed to the risk of changes in interest rates than longer-term bond funds yet offer more flexibility than GICs. You aren't locked into holding the fund for a set period and have the freedom to cash all or some of your investment at any time.

Some investors move money out of longer-term bond funds into short-term bond funds when interest rates appear set to rise. Trying to time movements in interest rates is difficult and not something we recommend.

Average MERs for short-term bond funds are typically less than for mortgage funds and longer-term bond funds.

Canadian bond funds

These funds make up the bulk of the bond funds available in Canada. Their main objective is to earn regular interest income on the money they invest. To do this they invest in bonds and debentures issued by governments, crown corporations, and private-sector corporations.

Most people should have some Canadian bond exposure in their portfolios. How much will depend on your age and how much regular income you need. Most Canadian bond funds distribute income either monthly or quarterly, but check this before you buy since some distribute income only once a year.

How well or poorly a bond fund will fare depends on various factors. Ultimately, these come down to the fund manager's ability to predict the trend in interest rates. But when picking a bond fund, you should be aware of three major differences between funds. These are:

• The term to maturity of the bonds in the fund. The average term-to-maturity of a bond fund is typically around 10 years. Funds with shorter average terms to maturity are typically safer, but they offer lower return potential. Funds with longer average terms, say 20 years, offer higher return potential but with higher risk. Fund managers will reduce or lengthen their average terms to maturity depending on their outlook for interest rates. If a manager believes interest rates are going to fall, then more money will be put

Term-to-maturity: *Amount of time left until a bond matures and its face value is paid back.*

Typical holdings by term

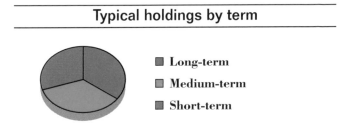

- ■ Long-term
- ■ Medium-term
- ■ Short-term

into longer-term bonds to capture a higher capital gain. When the outlook is for rising interest rates, the average term will be shortened. It's important to look at a fund's term-to-maturity before investing. You can usually get this information from the fund's statement of investment portfolio in its most recent financial statements. Several mutual fund analysis software packages will give you more recent term-to-maturity information.

Credit risk: *The risk that a bond issuer won't be able to pay you interest or return the bond's face value.*

- The credit quality of the bonds. Look at the proportion of federal government, provincial, corporate and other bonds. Some funds will invest exclusively in corporate bonds, making them riskier and potentially more lucrative than those that hold only higher quality government

Typical holdings by quality

- ■ Government of Canada
- ■ Provincial
- ■ Corporate

bonds, or a mix of government and corporate issues. While most funds restrict their investments to high-quality issues, the low interest rates of the past decade have prompted the emergence of a small number of so-called high yield funds. These funds seek to boost returns by taking on more credit risk, and may have little or no restrictions on the credit quality of portfolio holdings. In other words, they invest in what have come to be called "junk bonds." The potential gains — and losses — are greater in these high yield funds.

- The level of foreign currency denominated bonds in the portfolio. Foreign-pay bonds are issued by Canadian governments and companies, usually in U.S. dollars but sometimes in various European currencies, Japanese yen or Australian and New Zealand dollars. Even though they're denominated in foreign currency, these bonds still qualify as Canadian content in RRSPs. A fund that holds foreign-pay bonds might do so for two reasons. First, these bonds may pay higher rates of interest. Second, an anticipated decline in the Canadian dollar will make the interest payments and principal value of these bonds more valuable when translated into Canadian currency.

The cost of investing in bond funds varies considerably. Most funds carry MERs of less than 1.5%, with some far below 1% and others as high as 3%. You can start investing in a bond fund with as little as $25 although most ask for either $500 or $1,000 to start.

Foreign-pay bond:
A bond issued by a Canadian government or corporation denominated in a foreign currency.

Currency diversification:
Buying investments in different currencies to offset any weakening in one.

Foreign bond funds

These funds invest mostly in bonds denominated in a foreign currency. Foreign bond funds aim to provide you with income, safety and some potential for growth, as well as currency diversification. If the Canadian dollar weakens against other international currencies, then foreign bond funds will benefit.

Like Canadian bond funds, there can be term and quality differences between foreign bond funds. Some funds will invest in high quality bonds of governments and companies from around the world. Others will focus on higher yielding, riskier bonds from emerging markets. Some will invest in longer-term bonds with maturities of more than 20 years, while others are diversified between short, medium and long term bonds. Read and understand the fund's objective in the prospectus before buying a foreign bond fund.

Some foreign bond funds are considered

Typical holdings of foreign bond funds

■ Canadian foreign-pay   ■ European government
■ U.S. government   ■ Asian government
□ U.S. corporate   □ Emerging markets

Canadian content for registered plans such as RRSPs. By using foreign-pay bonds issued by Canadian governments and companies, the fund managers can bypass the 20% foreign-content limit. The most significant problem with this strategy is the sparse choice of securities and the higher credit risk.

The main use for foreign bond funds is to add diversity to your portfolio, reducing your risk exposure and giving you an opportunity to earn higher returns. However, you should be aware that a foreign bond fund can be significantly more expensive than a Canadian bond fund. This will show up in the average MER of 2%, which is typically 0.5% higher than for Canadian bond funds.

Balanced and asset allocation funds

Most investors should divide their investments across the three asset classes of cash, fixed income and equity, and also have some international diversification. This is what balanced and asset allocation funds aim to do – hold a diversified portfolio that balances risk and return.

The chief difference between balanced funds and asset allocation funds is how much freedom the managers have. Managers of balanced funds typically must hold a sizeable percentage of each asset class at all times. Asset allocation managers have free reign to "overweight" an asset class depending on which asset class they think is going to earn higher returns.

Overweight:
Having a higher than usual percentage of the portfolio invested in a specific asset class or sector.

However, even within each category, you will find differences. Balanced funds can be subdivided into Canadian, high income and global, while asset allocation funds may have tactical or strategic styles. This is explained in Chapter 6.

It's important to consider the MER when buying one of these funds. Fees can range from less than 1% to as much as 3.5%. The typical fee is about 2.5%. This relatively high fee structure reflects the fund manager's need for skills and support staff in both fixed-income and equity securities.

The idea behind balanced and asset allocation funds is for you to hold all your money in one fund rather than buy several funds across the asset classes. If you opt for this simplified approach, be sure to do your homework. Pick a fund that has a solid track record, where the mix of investments or the fund manager's strategy fits with your objectives, and make sure the fund has a reasonable MER.

Real Estate Investment Trust:
A trust that holds real estate and passes on most of its income to investors.

Royalty trust:
A trust that hold resources like oil and gas, from which profits flow to investors.

Canadian high-income balanced funds

These funds aim to maximize the amount of regular income they distribute to their unitholders. To do this, they invest in higher yielding investments like royalty trusts and real estate investment trusts (REITS). These funds invest in a mix of asset classes but hold at least 25% of their assets in interest-paying securities like bonds and 50% in non-interest but income-producing investments like preferred shares, high yield common stock and income trusts.

Global balanced and asset allocation funds

These hold a combination of foreign equity, foreign fixed-income investments, and foreign cash. It's hard to tell by the fund's name whether a foreign fund in this group is actually a balanced or asset allocation fund. Usually, they are not restricted in the mix of investments.

Canadian balanced funds

These funds hold a mix of cash, fixed-income securities and common stocks. The rough investment mix is explained in a fund's prospectus. It will tell you if the fund's bias is towards capital appreciation or income. If growth is the focus, then more of the portfolio will be in stocks. If the aim is income, then the fund will generally hold more bonds than stocks.

For most Canadian balanced funds, stocks should never make up more than 75% or less than

Typical holdings of Canadian balanced funds

■ Canadian equities ☐ Foreign bonds
■ Foreign equities ■ Canadian bonds
■ Cash

25% of the portfolio, and the same goes for bonds. The portfolio manager may change the proportion of stocks and bonds in the portfolio for short periods, but over the long-term the mix will stay fairly constant.

Fund managers of most Canadian balanced funds almost always try to invest to fit the investment objectives and temperaments of the most conservative investors. Typically, they invest only in blue chip stocks and the highest-rated bonds. The actual amount of each will depend on the manager's outlook for the markets.

Canadian asset allocation funds

Canadian asset allocation funds have an objective similar to balanced funds but the manager has the freedom to swing 100% into one asset class. At any

How asset allocation funds can change assets

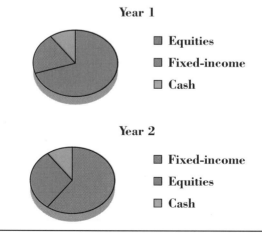

Year 1

■ Equities
■ Fixed-income
□ Cash

Year 2

■ Fixed-income
■ Equities
□ Cash

one time, the fund may hold only bonds or stocks if the fund manager is convinced that this is where he or she can get the best returns. Few managers would place such a heavy bet, but these funds have that leeway. The dynamic nature of asset allocation funds can make them riskier than balanced funds, since an incorrect move by the manager can hurt your returns. When you invest in one of these funds, you are in essence staking your faith on the manager's abilities to time the markets.

Fund sponsor: *Company that administers and markets a mutual fund.*

There are also asset allocation services available from fund companies that will shift your investments from fund to fund to match the fund managers' outlook or the conclusions of a computer-generated model. Sometimes called funds of funds, the sponsor often offers several fund combinations to meet different investment objectives. The fund combinations range from aggressive to conservative and any changes made to the asset allocation affect all investors using that particular portfolio.

Equity funds

Over the long term, stocks have historically offered better returns than other investments. Of course, together with these superior returns go greater risks. If you have a long investment horizon, then you will be able to ride out the dips in the market. But even older investors probably need at least some growth in their portfolios. Many of us will live longer than was possible in the past. This means we'll need our money to continue growing if we don't want to outlive it.

Most equity funds invest in common stocks, although some invest in preferred shares and other securities that can be turned into common shares. There are three big groups of equity funds — Canadian, foreign and global sector. These big groups can in turn be divided into smaller groups. In the Canadian equity group, fund types include dividend, large-cap and small- to-mid-cap, which hold stocks based on their market capitalization. In the foreign funds group you will find two main fund types — international funds, which invest outside Canada and the United States, and global funds, which invest in all of the world's major markets including North America. Within the third big group, global sector funds, you will find funds that target companies in specific industries and individual countries. Sector funds are often riskier because they are less diversified.

Since Canada is a small player in world markets, accounting for less than 3% of world stock trading, it's important to diversify internationally. Holding stocks from around the world gives you more opportunity to reduce risk and boost returns. World stock markets, and niches within those markets, tend to perform differently from our markets and also from each other.

However, you should be mindful of the risks of international investing. You could encounter political and economic instability or natural disasters. At the same time, some foreign stock markets are not regulated or monitored in the same

Preferred share:
A stock with limited voting power but which entitles you to a set amount of dividends before common shareholders get theirs.

Investment horizon:
Length of time you have to invest until you need your money.

way as in Canada and the United States. A loss of confidence in one of these markets can cause them to collapse, wiping out billions of dollars over a few days. Another risk arises from currency fluctuations. A strengthening in the Canadian dollar while you are invested abroad can eliminate any gains you might enjoy from the performance of the fund's investments.

If you are holding funds within a registered plan like an RRSP, the maximum foreign content you are allowed is 20% of the cost of all the investments in the plan. To avoid that limitation, fund companies have created funds that invest most of their money in money market securities and use derivatives, such as forwards and futures on foreign stock indices, to get exposure to foreign markets. This lets these funds remain fully eligible for registered plans. Another way to get foreign exposure is to buy equity funds that hold North American-based companies that have significant business in other countries.

Registered plan:
Plan registered with Revenue Canada in which investments can grow tax free until withdrawn.

Derivative:
A tradable contract that lets you buy or sell a security on a future date; rises and falls in value with the security's price changes.

Canadian dividend funds

For people with a low risk tolerance, but who want some exposure to equities, dividend funds might be the answer. These funds aim to provide income from dividends either monthly or quarterly. Since dividends are taxed at a lower rate than interest, getting income from dividend funds can mean you will get to keep more of the money you make. These funds are often viewed as alternatives to

Typical holdings of dividend funds

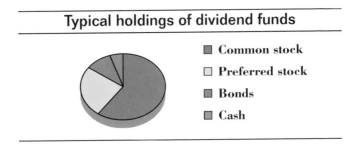

■ Common stock
□ Preferred stock
■ Bonds
□ Cash

bond funds, albeit riskier alternatives.

The funds invest mostly in common shares of large established companies that pay higher than average dividends and are therefore less risky investments. They also invest in preferred shares of Canadian companies. However, some dividend funds hold bonds — producing interest income that doesn't qualify for that special tax treatment. In fact, more than half of Canadian dividend funds are likely to hold bonds in their portfolio, with some allocating up to 20% to them.

Like bond funds, dividend funds are sensitive to changes in interest rates. When rates rise, their unit prices fall. However, the effect is less than with bond funds, because of the high proportion of common stocks in the portfolio. Common stocks also give these funds higher potential for capital growth. When stock markets are rising, dividend funds can do well, often outshining other types of equity funds.

MERs for dividend funds vary from just over 1% to 3%, with most in the 2% ballpark.

Global and international equity funds
You might be surprised to find global and

Typical holdings of international funds

☐ Japan   ■ Hong Kong
■ United Kingdon ☐ South America
■ Germany   ☐ Pacific Rim
■ France   ☐ Other Europe
☐ Italy

international equity funds ranked safer than most other stock funds, but it makes sense when you consider how geographically diversified these funds are.

The typically more diversified of the two are global equity funds. These invest most of their money in companies in each of the world's three biggest economic regions – the Americas, Europe and Asia. That means they will invest in Canadian and U.S. companies in addition to companies in developed markets like the United Kingdom, Germany, France, Japan, Hong Kong, and Australia. This widespread geographical diversification means these funds are not dependent on one economy for their returns. While companies in one or more countries might do

Geographic diversification: *Investing in a variety of countries to reduce risk and return dependence on any one country.*

Typical holdings of global funds

■ Foreign
■ Canada
☐ U.S.

poorly, companies in other regions might be doing better. This balances the fund's returns and reduces the overall risk in the portfolio.

International equity funds are much like their global counterparts, except that they don't invest in Canada and the U.S. This means these funds can lose out if the U.S. and Canadian stock markets perform well.

Sold with a variety of load options, these funds have MERs in the range of 2.5%, with lows of less than 1% and highs of more than 3.5%. Minimum first-time investments are usually set at about $500.

European equity funds

Investing in different European nations has allowed these funds to earn a reputation for relatively stable returns on average. Although their performance is broadly the same, economies of different European nations will perform differently in any given year. This gives fund managers the opportunity to earn higher returns if they can accurately forecast those countries that will perform best in a given year.

Most European equity funds invest in large

Typical holdings of European equity funds

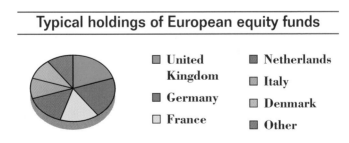

- United Kingdom
- Germany
- France
- Netherlands
- Italy
- Denmark
- Other

established companies in countries such as the United Kingdom, Germany, France, Italy, the Netherlands, and Denmark. Others focus on smaller companies in the modernizing economies of Eastern and Southern Europe.

Most of these funds qualify as foreign content in an RRSP. More than one country must be represented in the portfolio at all times. MERs are typically pegged at around 2.5%, while the average minimum investment is $500.

U.S. equity funds

These funds give you exposure to the world's largest economy. They typically invest at least half their money in larger U.S. companies in various industries.

Some U.S. equity funds are index funds, which means they hold most of their money in Canadian government T-bills and buy derivative contracts on U.S. indexes. Since these funds qualify as Canadian content in an RRSP, you can get U.S. exposure without affecting your 20% foreign content limit.

MERs for U.S. equity funds are typically

Index fund:
Fund that tries to match the performance of an index by holding component stocks or using derivatives.

Typical holdings of U.S. index funds

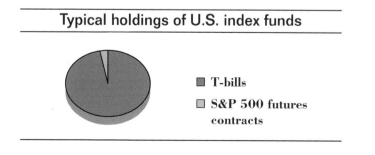

■ T-bills
□ S&P 500 futures contracts

---

around 2.3% with some index varieties offering MERs of less than 1%. First-time investments are typically in the range of $500 to $1,000.

North American equity funds

These funds mainly invest in a mix of Canadian and U.S. companies, with a minimum of 25% of the stocks in the portfolio dedicated to American companies. Some funds also invest in Mexican companies.

Because their foreign content exceeds the 20% that Revenue Canada allows for registered portfolios, these funds don't qualify as Canadian content in an RRSP, even though they may contain a high percentage of Canadian stocks.

Typical holdings of North American funds

■ U.S.

☐ Canada

■ Mexico

TSE 100:
An index of the biggest 100 stocks on the Toronto Stock Exchange.

Canadian large-cap equity funds

These focus on companies in Canada's TSE 100, an index that represents 100 of the largest companies listed on the Toronto Stock Exchange. These companies typically have average market capitalizations of more than $3 billion.

TSE 300

subindexes

1. Metals & minerals
2. Gold & precious metals
3. Oil & gas
4. Paper & forest products
5. Consumer products
6. Industrial products
7. Real estate
8. Transportation & environmental services
9. Pipelines
10. Utilities
11. Communications & media
12. Merchandising
13. Financial services
14. Conglomerates

Companies in the TSE 100 index are considered Canada's blue-chip companies. They are mature, well established and often have a history of solid returns and dividend payments over many years, if not many decades. The list includes companies that are household names across the country: the banks, BCE, Northern Telecom, Alcan and Imperial Oil. Most of these companies have a history of paying generous dividends. These dividends soften the changes in stock prices, giving a portfolio of mature companies a less volatile return.

MERs for large-cap funds are typically in the range of 2% to 2.5%. Initial minimum investments are pegged at $500 or $1,000 in most cases.

Blue chip:
The biggest, most solid companies; term taken from the most expensive chips in poker.

Canadian equity funds

This is the biggest category of funds in Canada with almost 250 different funds. The Canadian equity fund category concentrates its investments in a mixed bag of stocks of companies listed on Canadian stock exchanges. A broadly diversified fund will spread its holdings among many companies in a variety of industries and businesses, both small and large. For this reason, they are sometimes referred to as "mixed-cap" Canadian equity funds. Strictly speaking, a Canadian equity fund should hold companies in at least six of the 14 TSE 300 subindexes.

Typical holdings of Canadian equity funds

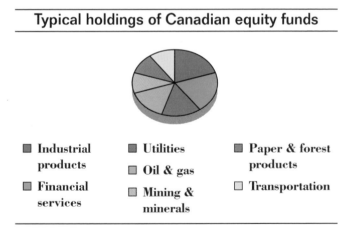

■ Industrial products	■ Utilities	■ Paper & forest products
■ Financial services	□ Oil & gas	□ Transportation
	□ Mining & minerals	

Most Canadian equity funds aim to match or beat the returns of the TSE 300. They are suitable as a core equity holding in a portfolio for investors of average risk tolerance.

However, there are style differences between

Canadian equity funds. These reflect the manager's approach to investing. Canadian equity funds can be categorized as growth-oriented or value-biased. These styles are explained in greater depth in Chapter 6.

MERs for Canadian equity funds vary widely from less than 1% to as much as 4%, although the average would appear to be about 2.25%. These funds are sold under a variety of load options, while the minimum initial investment typically is $500 or $1,000.

U.S. small- to mid-cap equity funds

These funds invest in smaller U.S. companies that have a market capitalization of less than U.S. $6 billion. Though more volatile than large-cap funds, these companies hold out the promise of higher than average growth. Typically, small-cap companies do not pay dividends and their shares are often expensive compared to their earnings.

Small-cap funds are suitable if you have a higher risk tolerance, a long time horizon and plan to include them as part of a larger equity portfolio that includes more stable large-cap funds. MERs

Small-cap: *Smaller, usually younger, companies whose shares have a total value under a certain amount.*

Typical holdings of small-cap funds

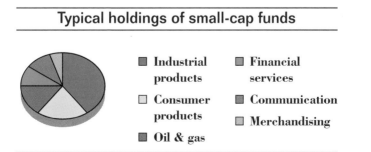

- Industrial products
- Consumer products
- Oil & gas
- Financial services
- Communication
- Merchandising

Micro-cap:
Highly speculative companies, usually technology firms with no revenues.

are typically in the range of 2.5%, with minimum initial investments around $500.

Canadian small- to mid-cap equity funds

Small-cap funds look for above-average growth in earnings from typically young Canadian companies that have market capitalizations of less than $1.5 billion. Stocks in these funds are riskier because they pay few if any dividends, choosing instead to reinvest their earnings to grow. Of course, greater potential risk goes with greater potential for growth.

There are a few mutual funds that invest only in "micro-cap" companies, sometimes putting their money only in companies with market values of less than $75 million. Managers of these funds believe the potential for gains is greatest from the smallest companies. Common sense tells you that this concentration makes the funds more volatile than those of funds that invest in the stocks of larger, well-established companies.

MERs for small-cap funds are typically around 2.4%.

Japanese equity funds

The world's second-largest economy has not enjoyed good times in the past decade or so. But if you think the market is in for a rebound, then these funds may deserve a place in your portfolio. The story of Japan's dismal stock market returns of the

1990s serves to illustrate the risk of investing in a single market, be it Japan, the U.S. or Canada. MERs for Japanese equity funds range from under 1% for index funds to over 3% for actively managed funds.

Global science and technology funds

Science and technology funds are one of the fastest-growing segments of the fund business.

They attract investors who see the best long-term returns in the future coming from knowledge-based companies. The science sector includes biotechnology, pharmaceuticals, medical devices and instrumentation. The technology sector includes computers, telecommunications, data processing and software industries.

Within this category you will find funds that invest in both science and technology companies, as well as those that focus on just one company type. Newer funds include those that focus on the telecommunications and the entertainment industries.

MERs for these funds vary, but are typically

Typical holdings of science & technology funds

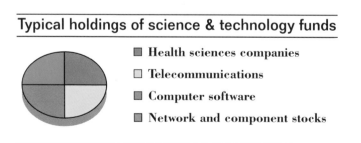

■ Health sciences companies

□ Telecommunications

■ Computer software

■ Network and component stocks

between 2% and 3.3%. First-time purchase limits range from $500 to $2,000.

Asia-Pacific Rim equity funds

These funds invest in companies in Asia, though often with the exception of Japan. Funds that exclude Japan are grouped in a category called Asia ex-Japan. If you already own a Japanese fund, you wouldn't want to buy an Asia fund that has additional Japanese content since this would increase your exposure to Japan.

Asia funds, often marketed as Far East funds, invest in a variety of countries in Southeast Asia and the Pacific Rim, including Hong Kong, Taiwan, Singapore, Australia and New Zealand, countries that at times have enjoyed dramatic economic growth.

These are high risk funds that have the potential to earn exceptional returns, but just as exceptional losses. They are suitable only as a small part of a broader portfolio.

MERs for Asia funds are typically around 2.75%, while first-time investments are typically either $500 or $1,000.

Typical holdings of Asia funds

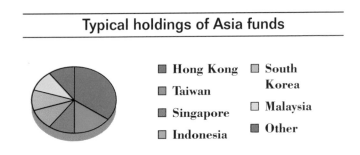

- ■ Hong Kong
- ■ Taiwan
- ■ Singapore
- □ Indonesia
- □ South Korea
- □ Malaysia
- ■ Other

Emerging markets equity funds

These funds invest in companies in less developed, high-growth regions around the world. Typically, this means companies in Southeast Asia, Latin America, and Eastern and Southern Europe. Investing in these markets is risky, but these funds try to diffuse the risk by spreading their investments over a wide variety of markets.

Typical holdings of emerging markets funds

- ■ South East Asia
- □ Latin America
- ■ Eastern and Southern Europe
- ■ Other

Emerging market funds are best held for the long term as part of a diversified equity portfolio that includes safer equity funds. This will soften some of the impact of the wild return variations that you can expect from emerging market funds from year to year.

MERs for these funds tend to be on the high side, ranging from 1% to almost 5%, with a median of about 2.8%.

Natural resources funds

Canada's stock markets are home to a large number of companies in the natural resources sector. For this reason, many natural resource funds are made up

Energy fund:
Fund that invests in companies in the oil and gas industry.

Economic cycle:
The natural flow of the economy through periods of growth and decline.

Typical holdings of a resource fund

- Mining & metals
- Oil & gas
- Forest & paper

mostly of Canadian stocks, which qualifies them to be held as Canadian content inside a registered plan.

Within this category you will find funds that invest in companies across the natural resource sectors, such as forestry and paper products, mining and oil and gas. Other funds specialize in only one sector, such as "Energy" funds that invest mainly in oil and gas companies.

Because of their narrow focus, these funds are high risk. Their returns are also tied to the cyclical fortunes of the resource industries, which go through periods of good returns and bad. For this reason, people often invest in these funds when they believe the resources sector is headed for good times, which is typically late in an economic expansion.

MERs for resource funds are typically in the region of 2.4%.

Latin American equity funds
A new fund category, Latin American funds invest in a wide variety of stocks, American depository receipts, derivatives and fixed-income investments of companies in Mexico, Central and South America and the Caribbean. The actual make-up of each

Typical holdings of Latin American funds

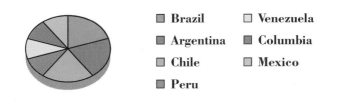

- ■ Brazil
- ■ Argentina
- ☐ Chile
- ■ Peru
- ☐ Venezuela
- ■ Columbia
- ☐ Mexico

American depository receipts (ADRs): *Receipts issued by U.S. banks and trust companies that trade on U.S. exchanges and which are equivalent to one share of a specific foreign company's stock.*

fund's portfolio will vary, so it's important to analyze this before buying one of these funds.

The countries these funds invest in represent some of the fastest growing economies in the world. However, there are high inherent risks to investing in these countries because they are prone to difficulties like high inflation, currency problems, high government debt, political instability and inefficient local securities markets. As a result, returns fluctuate widely, often from one month to the next.

MERs for these funds are typically just under 3%, which is relatively high. Minimum initial investments are pegged at $500 or $1,000.

Precious metals funds

Precious metals funds invest primarily in the stocks of Canadian gold mining companies. That means many of these funds can be held inside an RRSP or RRIF as Canadian content.

Returns on precious metals funds are closely tied to the performance of the physical metals. When gold prices are rising, these funds do particularly well. But when prices are falling, these

Typical holdings of a precious metals fund

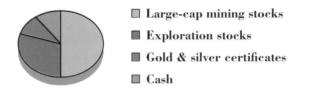

☐ **Large-cap mining stocks**
■ **Exploration stocks**
■ **Gold & silver certificates**
☐ **Cash**

funds lose money. For this reason, precious metals funds typically make up only a small part of a portfolio and are viewed as longer-term investments.

MERs for these funds are among the highest in the industry, sometimes more than 3%.

Country specific equity funds

These funds focus on specific countries. The most popular countries include India and Germany. Given the narrow concentration of these funds and the nature of some of these markets, these funds can offer great opportunity but at great risk.

MERs for these funds are high, sometimes more than 3%.

Other types of funds

Labor-sponsored venture capital corporations

As an incentive to invest in emerging opportunities and start-up situations, Canadian federal and provincial governments grant tax credits to investors in a mutual fund-like product called labor-sponsored venture capital corporations (LSVCCs). These funds are usually sponsored by unions and support such specific initiatives as job creation, small business, developments in a particular industry sector and economic revival in particular provinces. The investment manager of a labor-sponsored fund is usually hired by the fund sponsor for expertise in the fund's area of specialization.

Labor-sponsored funds are speculative investments. They invest in less-established ventures and have a tendency to do poorly in their early years. Another concern for managers of these funds is finding good investment opportunities within the time prescribed by Revenue Canada. A labor fund may be penalized for taking too long to invest its assets.

Book value:
What you originally paid for an investment, as opposed to its current market value.

Nonetheless, these funds are eligible for RRSPs and do offer the potential for long-term capital growth. Similar to a sector mutual fund, labor-sponsored funds offer limited diversification, making it important for you to diversify venture-capital holdings by using them as a small percentage — perhaps 5% or 10% — of your overall portfolio. Since labor funds qualify as "small business," you can use them to boost your self-directed RRSP's foreign content. For every $1 you hold in a labor fund, based on the original or book value, you can add $3 of foreign content — over and above the standard 20% limit. There's an overall cap or limit of 40% foreign content. So if you have $100,000 in your RRSP, your foreign content, at most, could be $40,000. Like choosing a mutual fund, selecting a labor-sponsored fund requires an examination of the fund's compatibility with your objectives, the track record of the manager in picking promising companies, and the manager's ability to meet the fund's objectives. You must consider the soundness of the fund as an investment, rather than focus on short-term incentives like tax savings.

The manager's expertise is especially important in a labor-sponsored fund. Investing in venture capital generally requires more work because venture companies are usually obscure and analyzing them is more difficult. These funds have high costs compared to mutual funds, which is reflected in their MERs of more than 4.5%.

Tax credits for LSVCCs

Labor funds offer combined federal and provincial tax credits of up to 30% (15% from each of the provincial and federal governments). While you can invest as much as you want in these funds, the credits apply to a maximum of $5,000 invested each year. You have to repay tax credits if you don't keep the investment for at least eight years. (For labor funds bought before March 6, 1996, you have to hold them a minimum of five years, or two years if you reach age 65, retire or cease to be a Canadian resident.)

Ethical funds

Ethical funds will hold only stocks and bonds of companies screened for social consciousness. They avoid companies involved in liquor, gambling or tobacco, and seek out companies that support environmentally sustainable economic development.

Real estate funds

We excluded these funds from our main fund list because of their somewhat dubious track record. While only a handful of real estate funds exist today, they were at one time a popular investment. This was before the real estate bust several years ago, when a flood of investors trying to cash in their units forced these funds to close redemptions.

Since many of these funds held their assets in real property and commercial buildings, they could not easily sell assets to raise the cash required to meet unitholders' demands for their money. In many cases, investors had to wait extended periods to be fully paid out, or had to sell their units after funds converted to closed-end funds that trade on stock exchanges.

Recently a couple of funds have been introduced which invest in the shares of real estate companies and trusts rather than in real property. These funds are less likely to have trouble meeting redemptions. However, you should think of them as potentially higher risk funds because their holdings are confined to a narrow asset type.

Summary table of mutual fund types

Money market	Canadian mortgage	Canadian short-term bond	Canadian bond	Foreign bond	Canadian high-income	Global balanced and asset allocation	Canadian asset allocation	Canadian balanced	Canadian dividend	Global + international equity	European equity	U.S. equity

Canadian money market

What they own* Government treasury bills, term-deposits, corporate notes.

What they aim to achieve Maximum security. Often used as a short-term investment.

Canadian mortgage

What they own* Minimum 75% of portfolio's market value must be invested in Canadian industrial, commercial and/or residential mortgages, including mortgage-backed securities.

What they aim to achieve Interest income and safety of principal.

Canadian short-term bond

What they own* No less than 75% of portfolio's market value must be invested in short-term Canadian debt securities such as bonds and mortgage-backed securities with a term to maturity of less than five years and more than one year.

What they aim to achieve Interest income and safety of principal. Because it stresses short-term holdings, there's less potential for interest rate trends to cause significant capital appreciation or loss compared to Canadian bond category.

Canadian bond

What they own* At least 75% of portfolio's market value must be invested in Canadian dollar-denominated government and/or corporate bonds, debentures and short-term notes. Average term to maturity of portfolio, including short-term investments, must be

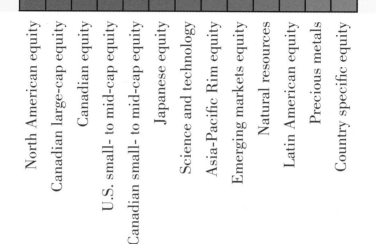

North American equity

Canadian large-cap equity

Canadian equity

U.S. small- to mid-cap equity

Canadian small- to mid-cap equity

Japanese equity

Science and technology

Asia-Pacific Rim equity

Emerging markets equity

Natural resources

Latin American equity

Precious metals

Country specific equity

greater than three years
What they aim to achieve Interest income and safety of principal. Can experience significant capital appreciation or loss depending on interest rate trends.

Foreign bond
What they own* At least 75% of portfolio must be in debt instruments denominated in a foreign currency and with a dollar-weighted term to maturity of greater than one year.

What they aim to achieve Safety of principal, income, capital appreciation. Buy bonds in high inflation countries for higher interest income and potential profit when inflation and interest rates fall.

Canadian high-income balanced
What they own*
Minimum of 25% of portfolio, including cash and equivalents, must be interest income-bearing securities and a minimum of 50% must be in non-interest,

but income-producing investments.

What they aim to achieve Dividend income, trust income, interest income and safety of principal.

Global balanced and asset allocation
What they own*
Portfolio must be invested in a combination of equity, fixed-income investments, cash and cash equivalents. At least 25% of investments must be non-Canadian. No

restrictions on asset weightings.

What they aim to achieve Similar to Canadian asset allocation, but using foreign investments.

Canadian balanced

What they own* At least 75% of portfolio's market value must be in a combination of Canadian equity and Canadian fixed-income. Equity portion must be no less than 25% and no more than 75% of portfolio. Fixed income and cash combined represent not less than 25% and not more than 75% of portfolio.

What they aim to achieve Mix of safety, income and capital appreciation. May shift money proportionately between asset types to reflect market conditions and outlook.

Canadian asset allocation

What they own* Minimum of 75% of the portfolio must be in one or a combination of Canadian fixed-income, Canadian equities or Canadian cash and equivalents. No restrictions on asset weightings or less stringent than for balanced funds.

What they aim to achieve Seeking the highest return, as opposed to sticking with a particular objective — safety, income or capital appreciation — sets this type of fund apart from the others. So at any given time, most of the portfolio may be invested in just one or two asset types, depending on market conditions and outlook.

Canadian dividend

What they own* Minimum 50% of total assets and 75% of non-cash assets must be dividend-paying securities of Canadian corporations, equity securities convertible into securities of Canadian corporations or royalty and income trusts (restricted to 25% of the portfolio) listed on a recognized exchange.

What they aim to achieve Tax-advantaged income.

Global & International equity

Global equity:
What they own* At least 50% of total assets and 75% of non-cash assets must be equities or equity equivalents of companies located in each of the three geographic regions of Asia, the Americas and Europe, or derivative-based exposure to such markets.

International equity:
What they own* Minimum 50% of total assets and 75% of non-cash assets must be equities or equity equivalents of companies located outside Canada and the U.S. or derivative-based exposure to such markets.

What they aim to

achieve Capital appreciation through foreign diversification.

European equity

What they own* At least 50% of total assets and 75% of non-cash assets must be equities or equity equivalents of European companies, or derivative-based exposure to developed European equity markets. More than one country must be in the fund at any time.

What they aim to achieve Capital appreciation through foreign diversification.

U.S. equity

What they own* At least 50% of total assets and 75% of non-cash assets must be equities or equity equivalents of companies located in the U.S. or derivative-based exposure to the U.S. market.

What they aim to achieve Capital appreciation, some income through dividends and stability

through broad diversification.

North American equity

What they own* At least 50% of total assets and 75% of non-cash assets must be equities or equity equivalents of companies located in the U.S. or Canada (or derivative-based exposure to those markets). U.S. equity portion must be at least 25% of the non-cash assets of the portfolio. Prospectus may allow them to hold as much as 100% U.S. equities.

What they aim to achieve Capital appreciation, some income through dividends and stability through broad diversification.

Canadian large-cap equity

What they own* Minimum 50% of total assets and 75% of non-cash assets must be in companies of the TSE 100 index, and with at

least 50% of equity weighting representing at least two of the four major subindexes of the TSE 100. Passive funds designed to track the TSE 300 Index are not included and are instead allocated to the Canadian equity category.

What they aim to achieve Capital appreciation, some income through dividends and stability through broad diversification.

Canadian equity

What they own* Minimum 50% of total assets and 75% of noncash assets in Canadian equities listed on a recognized stock exchange, and with significant holdings in companies of the TSE 300.

What they aim to achieve Capital appreciation, some income through dividends and stability through broad diversification.

U.S. small- to mid-cap equity

What they own* Minimum 50% of total assets and 75% of non-cash assets must be U.S. equities with a market capitalization of less than (U.S.) $6 billion.

What they aim to achieve Higher capital appreciation by seeking small- to medium-size companies with high growth prospects. More volatile than large-cap funds.

Canadian small- to mid-cap equity

What they own* At least 50% of total assets and 75% of equity holdings must be Canadian equities with a median market capitalization of not more than $1.5 billion.

What they aim to achieve Higher capital appreciation by seeking out small to medium-size companies with high growth prospects. More volatile than large cap funds.

Japanese equity

What they own* Minimum 50% of total assets and 75% of non-cash assets must be equities or equity equivalents of Japanese companies, or derivative-based exposure to Japanese equity markets.

What they aim to achieve Capital appreciation through foreign diversification.

Global science and technology

What they own* More than 50% of total assets and 75% of non-cash assets must be invested in equities or equity equivalents of companies primarily engaged in some aspect of science or technology.

What they aim to achieve Capital appreciation.

Asia/Pacific Rim equity

What they own* Minimum 50% of total assets and 75% of non-cash assets must be equities or equity equivalents of companies which are located in Asia, Australia or New Zealand, or derivative-based exposure to those markets.

What they aim to achieve Capital appreciation through foreign diversification.

Emerging markets equity

What they own* At least 50% of total assets and 75% of non-cash assets must be equities of emerging markets countries, or derivative-based exposure to such markets.

What they aim to achieve Capital appreciation through foreign diversification. More volatile than funds investing in developed markets.

Natural resources

What they own* At least 50% of total assets and 75% of non-cash assets must be invested in companies whose main business is tied to the exploration, extraction or production of natural resources, with no geographic restrictions.

What they aim to achieve Capital appreciation.

Latin American equity

What they own* More than 50% of total assets and 75% of non-cash assets must be equities or equity equivalents of companies located in Latin American countries, or derivative-based exposure to such markets.

What they aim to achieve Capital appreciation through foreign diversification. More volatile than funds investing in more developed markets.

Precious metals

What they own* More than 50% of total assets and 75% of non-cash assets must be invested in companies whose main business is tied to the exploration, extraction or production of precious metals, with no geographic restrictions.

What they aim to achieve Capital appreciation.

Country specific equity

What they own* At least 50% of total assets and 75% of non-cash assets must be invested in a specific country.

What they aim to achieve Capital appreciation, some income. Portfolio typically offers limited diversification.

*Allowable minimum and maximum percentage holdings based on median average values calculated from fund holdings over a period of three years. These definitions are based on draft proposals developed by the Investment Funds Standards Committee. The committee, made up of members of Canada's funds data publishing and analysis companies, was established in 1998 to create consistency in reporting mutual fund performance.

6

Fund
Managers'
Styles

K nowing how fund managers approach investing can help you identify funds that best fit your needs.

For many years, investors and analysts have concentrated on the kind of investments a portfolio manager chooses. More recently, mutual fund analysis has broadened to include a manager's investment style. Investment style is the approach the manager uses to choose investments.

Some managers begin the task of finding investments by looking at the financial, management and market strengths and weaknesses of individual companies. They focus squarely on the company and give only secondary regard to industry issues and economic analysis. This is

Bottom-up:
Analyzing a company before looking at its industry and the economy.

Top-down:
Analyzing the economy and industries before looking at companies.

called a bottom-up approach. They focus on the company's bottom line, then work their way up to the industry the company operates in and then to the broader economy.

Other managers work the opposite way. They start by looking at the big picture, such as which sectors of the economy they believe will generate above-average returns. Then they will look at particular companies or investments. This is called a top-down approach.

But neither the bottom-up nor the top-down approaches adequately describe what a manager looks for in the economy, an industry sector or an individual company. It also doesn't describe the different styles used by

A manager's starting point says much about their approach.

equity, fixed-income and asset allocation managers.

Understanding managers' styles is important. Some styles are potentially riskier than others and may perform differently under certain conditions. Others involve more trading, which can add to a fund's management costs. Without knowing what style a manager uses, you don't really know if that fund is suitable for you.

Equity management styles

Value investing

Unearthing undervalued companies is the key to this approach. The objective is to find companies that will pay an above average dividend, and which have good potential to make their share price grow. These managers are bottom-up stock pickers who spend most of their time conducting exhaustive research on the companies they are thinking of investing in. They tend to buy stock in a small number of companies and hold these for a long time.

Value managers buy out-of-favor stocks they believe have investment merits the rest of the market has overlooked. They wait for the market to recognize the companies' true value, then sell on the premise that the stocks no longer meet their criteria since they're no longer undervalued. Since the stock is often cheap for a reason, it can take some time for value managers to realize their targeted returns.

The value style tends to do better than other equity styles when stock markets are falling. However, when the markets are rising, the value approach generally gets modest results compared to other styles. Over the long term, though, value investing has produced returns virtually identical, if not better than growth investing.

A typical value equity fund portfolio

Number of Shares		Average Cost	Market Value	Percentage of Net Assets
Canadian Equity Securities				
1,234,200	Alberta Energy Company Ltd.	$ 32,892,393	$ 34,249,050	1.5%
1,648,500	Alcan Aluminium Ltd.	39,455,225	64,950,900	2.8
2,757,300	Anderson Exploration Ltd.	36,742,352	38,602,200	1.6
1,940,000	Bank of Montreal	97,554,428	122,899,000	5.2
2,224,352	Canfor Corporation	29,329,731	19,129,423	0.8
1,678,600	Cominco Ltd.	40,368,889	36,677,410	1.6
878,000	Co-Steel Inc.	14,075,639	16,682,000	0.7
764,800	Crestbrook Forest Industries Ltd.	11,184,626	3,824,000	0.2
1,722,100	Dofasco Inc.	27,741,945	39,608,300	1.7
2,400,000	Finning International Inc.	7,424,698	43,200,000	1.8
2,595,500	Fletcher Challenge Canada Limited, Class A	51,625,318	50,612,250	2.2
1,548,600	Le Groupe Vidéotron Ltée	16,791,408	19,357,500	0.8
1,405,300	Hudson's Bay Company	36,994,820	44,758,805	1.9
2,782,400	Inco Limited	106,673,385	67,612,320	2.9
1,176,000	Jannock Limited	16,185,841	21,756,000	0.9
3,144,900	Methanex Corporation	37,704,581	35,694,615	1.5
6,623,800	Nova Corporation	67,931,353	90,083,680	3.8
1,022,550	The Oshawa Group Limited, Class A	22,640,321	25,563,750	1.1
1,748,300	Provigo Inc.	15,403,137	15,210,210	0.7
2,368,000	Renaissance Energy Ltd.	65,096,857	69,856,000	3.0
1,002,000	Rigel Energy Corporation	13,978,538	11,723,400	0.5
985,500	Rio Algom Limited	25,722,946	23,799,825	1.0
3,117,900	Shell Canada Limited, Class A	43,105,820	80,130,030	3.4
1,672,797	Slocan Forest Products Ltd.	22,201,655	12,796,897	0.5
1,969,000	St. Laurent Paperboard Inc.	40,075,850	36,229,600	1.5
2,727,600	Sun Media Corporation	14,547,200	37,095,360	1.6
829,200	Talisman Energy Inc.	24,846,353	36,277,500	1.5
1,805,900	Tarragon Oil and Gas Limited	22,078,283	20,226,080	0.9
2,177,000	Teck Corporation, Class B	50,890,828	46,914,350	2.0
815,300	Teleglobe Inc.	15,373,407	35,465,550	1.5
1,400,000	Trimac Limited	5,359,813	14,420,000	0.6
1,083,300	Westaim Corporation	4,505,597	7,745,595	0.3
1,739,100	Westburne Inc.	18,977,352	27,825,600	1.2
423,000	West Fraser Timber Co. Ltd.	12,709,451	15,016,500	0.6
	Securities being acquired / disposed of	41,344,493	44,257,016	1.9
		1,129,534,533	1,310,250,716	55.7
Foreign Equity Securities				
1,200,000	Chrysler Corporation	53,870,176	60,403,405	2.6%
761,200	Circus Circus Enterprises, Inc.	25,938,535	22,322,581	1.0
232,400	Eastman Kodak Company	18,451,333	20,217,188	0.9
832,000	ITT Industries, Inc.	26,518,029	37,342,107	1.6
270,000	King World Productions, Inc.	14,856,201	22,305,271	0.9
1,055,100	Mallinckrodt, Inc.	52,922,678	57,354,696	2.4
817,200	Polaris Industries, Inc.	27,271,105	35,728,024	1.5
1,726,600	Silicon Graphics, Inc.	50,553,615	31,182,784	1.3
612,800	Sterling Software, Inc.	23,559,071	35,941,349	1.5
250,000	Tecumseh Products Company, Class A	19,185,602	17,434,375	0.7
841,500	Toys "R" Us, Inc.	28,619,550	37,843,725	1.6
12,474,000	United Biscuits (Holdings) PLC	58,745,695	65,757,696	2.8
612,800	Zilog, Inc.	16,665,708	16,710,536	0.7
	Securities being acquired / disposed of	1,124,083	1,544,283	0.1
		418,281,381	462,088,020	19.6
		1,547,815,914	1,772,338,736	75.3
Precious Metals				
279,940	Gold certificates	124,323,237	115,752,317	4.9
		124,323,237	115,752,317	4.9
Bonds and Convertible Debentures				
$ 350,000	Emco Limited, Convertible debenture, 7.25%, April 30, 2002	348,299	346,500	0.0
27,000,000	Government of Canada, 6.25%, September 15, 1998	27,876,800	27,240,300	1.2
		28,225,099	27,586,800	1.2
		1,700,364,250	1,915,677,853	81.4
	Short-term investments	419,088,192	419,088,192	17.8
	Total cost and market value of investments	2,119,452,442	2,334,766,045	99.2
	Other assets (net)	18,076,512	18,076,512	0.8
	NET ASSETS	$ 2,137,528,954	$ 2,352,842,557	100.0%

Value managers believe less is more and typically hold about 50 stocks.

Since value stocks typically pay higher dividends proportionate to their share prices, they are less volatile and their share prices tend to rise and fall less than other stocks. Another reason for this relative stability is that value stocks are already priced low, so the potential for a further decline is low. This reduced volatility, plus the dividend income, makes value funds attractive to more conservative investors.

Finding value stocks starts with the mathematical task of screening companies' financial results. Value investors use a number of financial ratios in their analysis. Many of these ratios compare the current share price to figures like the company's profits. A common ratio used is the price-earnings (P/E) multiple, which compares how much earnings are behind the company's share price. The ratio tells a manager how expensive a stock is compared to other stocks. The lower the P/E multiple, the cheaper the stock.

Another commonly used ratio is the dividend yield. It calculates the annual dividend payments as a percentage of the share price, almost like calculating interest. The higher the yield, the cheaper the stock. For value managers, the more profit, dividends or cash flow backing each share of a company the better.

Value investors will also look at other "assets" that don't appear on the balance sheet. These include strong management, exceptional products, trademarks or a strong competitive position within the industry.

P/E multiple: *How many times a common stock's annual earnings per share can be divided into the current share price. Tells you how expensive a share is.*

**Dividend
yield:**
*A common
stock's
annual
dividend
stated as a
percentage
of the
current
share price.*

Since value managers tend to hold onto the stocks they eventually buy, their funds have what's called low portfolio "turnover." This means they pay less over time for expensive research and commissions and other transaction costs. This lower cost means value equity funds typically have lower MERs. It will also mean less frequent realized capital gains, which can be an advantage if your returns are taxable. This occurs because capital gains are triggered only when an investment is sold – and value managers don't sell as often as other managers. This effectively postpones your taxes. When they do sell, however, the capital gains can be substantial.

One drawback of the value approach is that proponents of this style, adhering too strictly to their value criteria, will sometimes overlook companies

Value vs. Growth

Value	Growth
• Out-of-favor stocks	• Hot stocks
• Fewer holdings	• Many holdings
• Hold long-term	• Hold medium term
• Lower P/E	• Higher P/E
• Higher dividend yield	• Lower dividend yield
• Lower costs	• Higher costs
• Infrequent capital gains	• Frequent capital gains
• Less market timing	• More market timing
• Less volatile	• More volatile

with good growth potential. They might also mistakenly pick companies with cheap fundamentals only to find that the companies need to overcome impossible financial or competitive difficulties.

Growth investing

Growth managers are unabashed capital gains hunters. They target companies with strongly growing earnings with the idea of turning a short- to mid-term profit when share prices ramp up. The manager looks for companies with "earnings momentum," meaning profitable companies that appear destined for even higher profits. Growth managers are less concerned than value managers about ratios like P/E multiples. Their philosophy is that it's better to pay more for firms whose growth potential justifies a higher price than to pay less for a company with questionable growth prospects.

You can expect this kind of portfolio to have high P/E multiples. Compared to value stocks, that means growth stocks have less profit behind each share. However, the manager's focus is on the company's future earnings growth, so a high current P/E might be justified if future earnings are going to increase substantially. Growth managers will also try to identify companies with competitive advantages, such as advanced proprietary technology. They also generally favor less-established companies. In theory, the higher prices and stronger fundamentals that usually distinguish growth stocks are justified by the imminent growth of the company.

Cash flow:
A company's profits plus "expenses" that aren't actually paid out in cash, such as owed taxes that will only be paid in future.

A typical growth fund portfolio

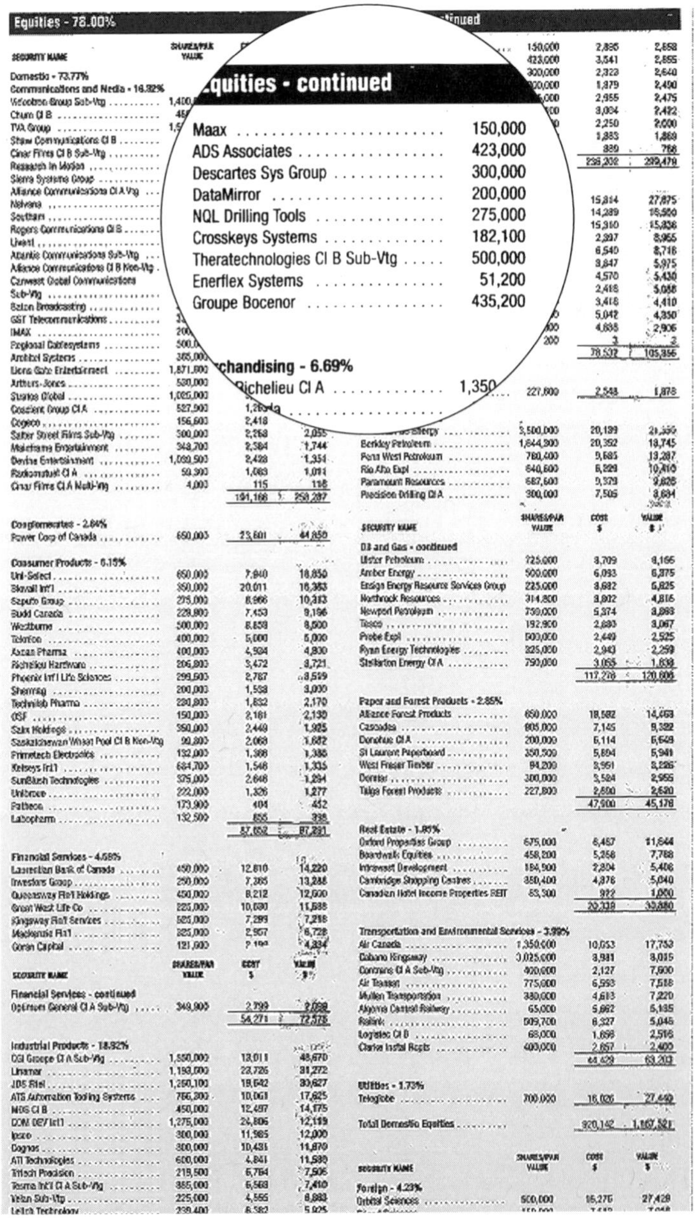

Equities - 78.00%

SECURITY NAME	SHARES/PAR VALUE		

Domestic - 73.77%
Communications and Media - 16.32%

Equities - continued

Maax	150,000
ADS Associates	423,000
Descartes Sys Group	300,000
DataMirror	200,000
NQL Drilling Tools	275,000
Crosskeys Systems	182,100
Theratechnologies Cl B Sub-Vtg	500,000
Enerflex Systems	51,200
Groupe Bocenor	435,200

...chandising - 6.69%

Richelieu Cl A 1,350

Growth funds often have more than 150 separate holdings.

In some ways, growth managers are impatient investors. They tend to buy many more companies' stocks than do value managers. This they do in the hopes of having more good stocks than bad ones, and also to reduce dependence on any one stock or group of stocks. The portfolio may also be turned over more often than with value funds. This tends to slightly increase trading costs and therefore the average expenses you pay to the fund. If the growth manager is also a "momentum" investor – quickly selling stocks if the company's earnings are disappointing or the stock price falls, for any reason – then the fund may be even more expensive to run. This turnover may also trigger more capital gains, and a higher tax bill for investors whose returns are taxable.

Growth funds are more susceptible to negative economic conditions or poor earnings results from the companies they own. This is because the shares they buy pay a lower percentage of dividends and are relatively expensive compared to their current earnings. If earnings fall, this can cause a sharp drop in your fund's value. This type of investing is also more vulnerable to market cycles. It can outperform in an up market, but tends to get hit harder in down markets. It is also volatile when actual earnings are reported above or below what analysts predicted. Growth companies reinvest their earnings which means they seldom pay dividends. This not only makes growth funds unsuitable for investors looking for income, it adds to the fund's

Portfolio turnover: *The rate at which a manager completely changes the stocks in a fund's portfolio.*

Analyst: *An expert who works for a brokerage or a fund who analyzes companies for investment.*

volatility since dividend income can stabilize returns in a portfolio.

Although they are a little riskier, growth funds also have more potential for medium-term capital appreciation than value funds.

Snapshot

sector rotators

- Top-down approach
- Look for economic trends
- Choose growth sectors
- Market timers
- Pick large-cap stocks
- Have many holdings
- High costs

Sector rotation

Sector rotators seek capital gains using a top-down approach. They analyze the prospects for the economy as a whole, then invest in those industry sectors expected to outperform the overall stock market. In picking the companies, the managers will use either a growth or value style or a blend of both.

When it appears that another industry is ready to outperform, the manager moves into that industry. This is known as sector rotation and it is generally considered extremely difficult to do consistently.

Sector rotators generally invest in the leaders of a particular sector. However, because investments are bought and sold as the economy moves through its cycle, portfolio turnover tends to be high. This pushes up trading costs, which tends to increase the expenses you end up paying to the fund. Also, this style can increase the amount of capital gains triggered and, as a result, the amount of taxes that you might be liable to pay each year.

Indexing

Indexing is a passive management style. The manager doesn't analyze individual companies but simply buys the same companies that are found in a well-known market index. Rather than earning higher returns, the manager's objective is to mirror the index's return as much as possible.

NASDAQ: *National Association of Securities Dealers Automated Quotations system; the electronic trading system that is the second-largest U.S. securities market.*

Commonly used indexes include the TSE 300, a grouping of 300 widely traded stocks on the Toronto Stock Exchange. A well-known U.S. index is the Standard and Poor's (S&P) 500. Some funds aim to match a market niche, such as the technology-heavy NASDAQ 100 index, while others use the combined performance of several markets as a benchmark.

The difference in MERs between index funds and actively managed funds can be significant. This is because changes to the structure of a market index are infrequent, so index managers don't buy and sell stocks as often as other managers. This results in low portfolio turnover and means lower management and trading costs, and a potential tax advantage.

Indexing can be used to boost foreign exposure above Revenue Canada's 20% limit for registered retirement accounts such as RRSPs. This is possible through index funds that use derivatives instead of buying the actual stocks in an index. These funds use a combination of safe Canadian government T-bills and derivative contracts on a foreign index. These derivatives give the fund the same exposure to the index as a stock-based index fund, but with a much smaller investment than buying the stocks themselves. Derivative-based index funds are fully eligible for registered plans like RRSPs because most of their money is held in Canadian T-bills.

However, you should remember that Revenue Canada treats the returns on derivative-based index funds as more heavily taxed interest income rather than tax-advantaged capital gains. This is why it might be better to hold derivative-based index funds inside your RRSP where they are

Index:
A statistical tool that measures the state of the stock market based on how component stocks perform.

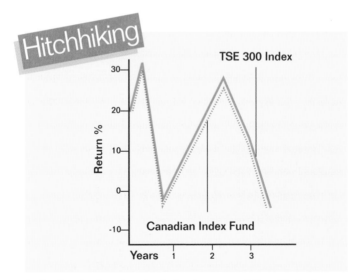

Index funds often lag the index because of the effect of management expenses. Beware that there may be wide variations in how well an index fund tracks its benchmark. You should check its tracking error history before buying.

sheltered from tax. If you are holding an index fund outside a registered plan, then stock-based index funds may be better because taxes are based on the lower rates for capital gains and dividends.

Index managers don't aim to outperform the market and — after fees and expenses — an index fund rarely will. On the other hand, this might not be a bad thing since few fund managers can consistently outperform the market. Theoretically, though, index funds are more vulnerable in a plunging market than funds protected by the expertise of an active manager. The manager of an actively managed fund can take evasive action to reduce losses in a downturn, while index funds spiral down along with the market benchmark.

Using a combination of investment styles

Many fund managers use a blend of styles in managing a portfolio. They might combine value and growth styles to get a mix of reasonably priced stocks that have growth potential. Others may blend top-down analysis with a value style, starting with the economy and promising industry sectors before subjecting individual companies to scrutiny for strict value criteria.

In fact, a few funds manage portions of their portfolio by different styles to achieve so-called style diversification. You can do this yourself by investing some of your money in a value oriented fund and the rest in a growth oriented fund. Over the long-term, however, studies show that value investing may get higher returns than growth

Market cycle: *Natural rise and fall of the market as it goes through good and bad economic conditions.*

investing, but the difference is slight. In the shorter-term, style diversification may reduce the risk of one style doing poorly during different stages of the market cycle. The disadvantage is that the weak performance of one style can reduce the strong performance of another.

Balanced and asset allocation styles

Strategic asset allocation

Many balanced fund managers use strategic asset allocation to keep to a fairly stable mix of equities, fixed-income and cash. The amount of each asset class in the mix is fixed within certain ranges, reflecting the manager's long-term expectations for which combination of the three asset classes will produce the return and risk best suited to an average conservative investor.

There are different ways to estimate future returns on the three main asset types. Investment management firms often use sophisticated models to do this. Security prices can also be forecast using historical returns. Stocks have historically produced the highest average returns over the long-term. Fixed-income investments like bonds historically have earned lower long-term returns than stocks, while safe cash investments like treasury bills have generated the lowest returns.

Another important feature of the three different asset classes is that they generally perform well at different times. When stocks are doing well, bonds are doing less well and cash assets even more poorly. But when stocks are dropping, bonds are generally rising. That's why a balanced fund manager who chooses an asset allocation of 70% equity, 20% fixed-income and 10% cash can expect to earn a higher return over the long-term, but with a higher level of risk to the portfolio because of the heavy equity weighting. An allocation of 45% equity, 45% bonds and 10% cash would be expected to lead to a more balanced long-term return because of the equal weighting of equities to fixed-income securities.

Strategic asset allocation: *Setting a mix of the three asset classes and sticking to it over the long term.*

Once a manager settles on the fund's strategic asset allocation, the mix will remain much the same over time. There will, however, be times when the weighting of one or more asset classes falls out of line with the strategic mix. This might happen due to a particularly strong or weak performance in one of the asset classes. Generally, managers will rebalance their portfolios when there is a 5% variance in their strategic allocation.

Tactical asset allocation
In contrast to many balanced fund managers, asset allocation funds generally use a tactical asset allocation approach. Tactical asset allocation managers typically have leeway to make wholesale short-term shifts between asset classes before returning the portfolio back to its strategic mix. A manager who believes stocks are

Tactical asset allocation: *Shifting away from a strategic mix for short periods to exploit market events.*

Rebalance: *Return a portfolio to its strategic asset mix.*

ready for a big fall would generally move more heavily into fixed-income and cash assets.

If the manager's call on the market is the right one, then the fund will record superior returns. Of course, if the prediction is wrong, then the fund could be staring at large losses or, at the very least, a missed opportunity.

Tactical asset allocation is grounded in the belief that the ups and downs of the stock and bond markets can be anticipated. In reality, though, it's extremely rare if not impossible for managers to consistently make correct calls on the market. They may be right on some occasions, but they will likely make the wrong move on others. This means tactical asset allocation typically leads to more volatility in the portfolio. However, this increased risk generally does not lead to higher returns in the long-term. In a 1998 Canadian Securities Institute study of historical mutual fund returns in Canada, it was found that asset allocation fund managers typically did not compensate investors with higher returns for the extra risk.

Still, this doesn't mean you should write off all tactical asset allocation funds. There are always exceptions. You may discover a fund manager who has been able to compensate investors with higher returns. Indeed, the same study that criticizes asset allocation managers also finds that managers who find a winning formula tend to repeat their good performance in future years.

Diary of a tactical asset allocation manager

% of portfolio

Year	Cash	Fixed-income	Equities	Remarks
	5	30	65	This is the model asset allocation.
1	5	20	75	Economy in early expansion phase of business cycle. Outlook good for stocks. Overweight stocks.
2	5	20	75	Outlook continues to be good for stocks. Economy in late expansion phase.
3	20	25	55	Inflationary pressures forcing up short-term interest rates. Overweight cash and short-term bonds. Economy has peaked.
4	5	40	55	Interest rates falling as economy begins to stall. Medium-term emphasis in fixed-income portfolio.
5	5	40	55	Early contraction stage. Recession conditions are apparent. Longer-term emphasis in fixed-income portfolio. Interest rates falling.
6	0	40	60	Late contraction stage. Interest rates continue to fall. Manager starts to shift back into equities.
7	5	30	65	Stock market trough. Shorter-term emphasis in fixed-income portfolio. Heavy shift to equities.
8	5	20	75	Economy in early expansion phase of business cycle. Outlook good for stocks. Overweight stocks.
9	5	20	75	Outlook continues to be good for stocks. Economy in late expansion phase.
10	5	30	65	New manager takes over. Decides outlook for stocks less favorable, and shifts to model asset allocation.

Fixed-income management styles

Fixed-income funds earn their returns from a combination of regular interest payments and capital gains. Since interest rates are a key factor in fund performance, adding value to a portfolio is mostly a matter of understanding the interest rate trend and managing risk.

Spread trading

Spread trading: *Exploiting small pricing differences to enhance returns in a bond portfolio.*

Spread trading is switching from one bond to another to take advantage of small pricing differences that sometimes occur in the market. Sometimes bonds that have close similarities can trade at different prices. By finding these mismatched pricings, the fund manager hopes to make a profit by later selling the bond at its true value. Spread traders must have thorough knowledge of the credit rating of various bonds and understand interest rate trends to recognize opportunities. These managers are active traders, which can lead to higher costs.

Term to maturity

Some bond funds restrict a manager to a specific term-to-maturity for the portfolio, with the fund prospectus setting out the risk constraints and investment restrictions. A five-year average term-to-maturity is common for funds that use this style.

A fund that maintains a term-to-maturity is an alternative to GICs and other investments of the same term. Bond funds, however, have greater flexibility

Long + short of it

Term	Years
Long	10 yrs+
Medium	3 to 10 yrs
Short	up to 3 yrs

since you can sell them when you want, unlike a typical fixed-term GIC. This characteristic makes funds with term-to-maturity restrictions especially suitable for conservative investors seeking income and not concerned about capital gains.

Term investment: *An investment where you commit to leaving your money on deposit for a set period in return for a guaranteed rate of return.*

Credit quality

Bond fund managers can choose from bonds issued by federal, provincial and municipal governments, and by corporate bond issuers. The quality of these bonds can range from speculative to high quality, as determined by the issuer's creditworthiness. Bonds of lower credit quality offer higher yields to compensate investors for their increased risk. Because of this, corporate bonds mostly have higher yields than comparable bonds issued by the Government of Canada, which is seen as having little chance of going bankrupt because of its ability to levy taxes.

Managing a bond portfolio using credit quality is a relatively aggressive approach. Some bond funds specialize in high-yield, low-quality issues called junk bonds. The risk with junk bonds is that the company won't be able to pay interest or repay the bond's face value. The flip side, of

Junk bond:
*High-risk
bond of a
heavily
indebted
company or
country that
might not be
able to meet
its
payments.*

Junk bonds pose significant bankruptcy risk.

course, is that managers can earn higher returns
on high-yield bonds in times when the risk of
companies defaulting is low, such as when
corporate earnings are stable or rising and the
economy is healthy.

Indexing

An indexing strategy for fixed-income funds is
very similar to indexing in a stock fund. It also
involves buying and holding a portfolio of
securities, in this case bonds instead of stocks,
that reflect a benchmark index. However, because

it's harder to replicate the securities that make up a bond index, the manager is forced to use bond issues that are as close as possible to the securities in the index.

Indexing is a low-cost, passive strategy for investing in the fixed-income markets. This strategy can be more effective for bonds than stocks because there are fewer opportunities for active bond managers to add value to their portfolios. Also, the lower costs of indexing will also contribute to higher returns for a given level of risk.

Interest-rate anticipation
Bond prices move in opposite directions to changes in general interest rates. When rates fall, bond prices rise and vice versa. Long-term bonds normally respond more sharply than shorter-term bonds when interest rates change.

Managing through interest rate anticipation involves lengthening the average term-to-maturity of a portfolio when interest rates are expected to fall, and shortening the term when interest rates are expected to rise. A manager who expects rates to fall across the board can make the biggest capital gain by lengthening the portfolio's average term-to-maturity by shifting money into longer-term bonds. Managers who use this technique scrutinize economic growth, political developments and monetary policy, which combine to affect interest rates.

One advantage of these funds is that the

credit quality of the investments is usually high. Holding high quality bonds makes it easier to make quick shifts between bonds of different terms. One disadvantage is the volatility caused by the unpredictable movements in interest rates. To use this management style successfully, a manager must not only be right when predicting the direction of interest rates, but also properly time these movements. This is difficult to achieve.

How the interest rate cycle affects the bond market

Stage in economic cycle and characteristics of each stage		Interest rate pattern	Bond market reaction
Expansion	Healthy growth, supply and demand are in balance	Stable rates until late stage	Yields rise slowly and bond prices begin to decline
Peak	Bottlenecks in supply and inflationary cost pressures	Rates rise as peak approaches	Prices drop quickly and yields reach cyclical peak
Contraction	Rising costs lead to cuts in production, growth stalls	Rates fall with drop in demand	Bull market for bond prices begins, anticipating recovery
Trough	Falling costs lead to resurgence in demand	Cyclical low for rates	Prices will be up from the lows and yields decline
Recovery	Growth resumes, economy regains lost income	Stay low until growth picks up	Yields steadily rise as bond prices rise to cyclical peak

Duration switching

The duration of a bond is not the same as its term-to-maturity, although it is also expressed in years. Essentially, duration is simply a way to measure how strongly a bond will react to small rather than large changes in interest rates. (A bond with a duration of 10 years will be more volatile than one with a duration of nine years.) Calculating the duration of a bond requires using a complex formula that factors in such things as the level and frequency of a bond's regular interest payments as well as the number of years until it matures. Duration is always less than or equal to a bond's term-to-maturity. The higher the interest rate on the bond and the more frequently interest is paid, the shorter its duration generally is. That means that two 10-year bonds may have different durations.

Duration switching involves trying to anticipate interest rate trends and picking the best duration to get maximum benefits with the minimum interest rate risk. However, this kind of strategy involves intense monitoring of markets and holdings, resulting in greater costs than low-turnover strategies.

The Art
of Fund
Selection

Picking the right funds for you is a painstaking and methodical process.

Tools of the fund sleuth

There are two basic ways to go about selecting a mutual fund. The first is to enlist the services of a competent financial advisor. The second is for you to do your own research. With about 2,000 individual funds to choose from, picking funds yourself can be a daunting task if you don't have access to a computer that's connected to the Internet or loaded with a custom mutual fund software program. While you could use one or more of the mutual fund guides published each year, you will still be relying on someone else's recommendations, as well as potentially dated information.

However, with a computer and a small investment in a mutual fund software program, you can be your own analyst and seek out funds using up-to-date and detailed data. In addition, there are free Web sites, such as The Fund Library (www.fundlibrary.com) and GlobeFund (www.globefund.com), that are good resources for the amateur fund analyst. They let you compare funds by key criteria, download prospectuses and read analysts' opinions on individual funds.

However, for in-depth information, you will need a paid subscription to a professional mutual fund data service. These include BellCharts, Globe HySales, PALTrak and Southam SourceDisk. Of these, the most widely used are BellCharts and PALTrak. Both of these products have a software engine and a vast store of data that is updated monthly by diskette or over the Internet. The software engine gives you the power to filter and compare funds using a variety of criteria. You can analyze funds' holdings, MERs, risk parameters and returns over various periods, to list only a few of the many features.

BellCharts and PALTrak are similarly priced, in the range of $200 for the initial software and four quarterly updates, or $400 for monthly updates. Competition is fierce between these providers, so look for special promotional offers that are often available. Both companies offer free product demos, which are great if you are planning to pick funds to hold for the long-term and won't be needing the software again for a few years. However, if you have a large portfolio that you plan to actively manage, then getting a full subscription to one of these services is a worthwhile investment.

Another source for fund analysis and information are brokerages that provide clients access to online trading. These companies often provide mutual fund analysis tools as part of the online service at no charge. Newspapers like The Globe and Mail and the National Post are also good sources of information, especially their special monthly mutual fund surveys.

Devise a method for your analysis

Picking a mutual fund is a process. The first step in your research is to identify which broad category of fund you want to buy. Will it be Canadian or international? An equity, fixed income or money market fund? And even within these three asset classes, which particular types of funds are you interested in? You will, of course, be guided in this by your personal investment goals and risk tolerance.

Your next steps are to analyze in great depth a fund's risk and return profile. These two measures — risk and return — are your primary concerns. Secondary issues you should consider are the funds' portfolio composition, fee structure and tax efficiency. Put together in one sentence, the process seems quick and easy. But proper analysis is a time consuming process. It starts with a large number of funds and slowly eliminates potential

Tax efficiency: *How a fund's distributions will be taxed in your hands.*

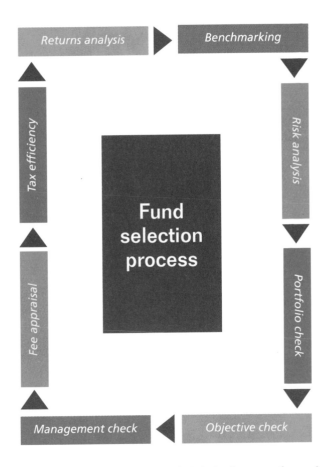

Developing a method for your analysis helps keep you focused on your objective, i.e. to find the best fund for your needs.

candidates until you arrive at the one fund that best captures your needs.

Your ultimate objective is to find funds that will help you achieve your objectives with the least possible risk. When all is said and done, all types of investing come down to a matter of balancing risk and return to achieve your goal.

Remember, too, that you will perform this process of whittling down a large number of funds to a single eligible fund at least four times. This is because a properly constructed portfolio will consist of funds from each of the equity, fixed-income and cash classes, with some international equity exposure as well.

Analyze fund returns

You've seen the warnings on mutual fund ads: "Past performance is no guarantee of future performance." That's true, but with nothing else to go by, history may be your best tool to assess a mutual fund's future potential. Research also shows that fund managers appear to be quite consistent in their performance over time. However, past returns must be used with care.

Annual return: *The return on an investment from the beginning to the end of a 12-month period.*

When comparing fund returns, make sure you are comparing apples with apples. It doesn't make sense to compare an equity fund to a bond fund. Even differences within fund types can make them unsuitable for comparison. A Canadian equity fund that invests in a broad range of large companies is different from one that invests in the shares of a limited number of small-cap companies.

Fund performance should be reviewed over longer periods of at least five years, but preferably 10 years. And you should use both the fund's annual and compound average returns to measure performance.

Know the returns you're comparing

Mutual fund companies report returns in several ways, so it's important to know what returns you're looking at when comparing funds. It's often a good idea, too, to compare funds using different return criteria to get a clearer picture of how the funds stack up.

Positive return:
A return greater than or equal to zero.

Annual returns

These are a fund's returns over consecutive 12-month periods. Annual returns, sometimes called calendar returns, are typically calculated to December 31 and measure a fund's performance as if a unit was bought on January 1. The return includes dividends or interest distributed to

---

Look for stable, positive returns

What you *do* want to see

2000	1999	1998	1997	1996	1995
17.5	10	9	15	3	8

$1,000 invested in this fund earns $802.25 in six years.

What you *don't* want to see

2000	1999	1998	1997	1996	1995
19	-36	37	30	21	-17

$1,000 invested earns just $362.24 in six years, despite outperforming Fund 1 in four of the six years.

---

unitholders. If $1,000 invested at the start of the year grows to $1,100 at year-end, then the annual return on the investment is 10%.

Annual returns are useful because they give you insights into the performance of one fund compared to another in specific years. They also show you how volatile a fund is from year to year. Ideally, you want a fund where returns are consistently above average, with low fluctuations from one year to the next. With some fund categories, such as money market funds, this consistency is commonplace. In equity and fixed-income funds, though, consistent positive returns are rare. Almost all funds will have a poor year in a 10-year period.

Compound returns: *A method of calculating average returns for a period which masks the best and worst returns during the period.*

Compound average annual returns

Compound average annual returns are typically calculated for three-, five- and 10-year periods. There is a danger to looking at compound returns alone because they smooth out the highs and lows in a fund's performance. A chronic poor performer that happened to do well in the most recent year

Compound returns hide volatility

5-year compound return

Year 1	Year 2	Year 3	Year 4	Year 5	
11.2%	18.1%	9.7%	52.5%	5.9%	= 17.4%

If not for the high return in Year 4, this fund would have had a much lower five-year compound return.

may look good if you judge it only by its compound average return. This would be exactly the kind of fund to avoid if you're a long-term investor.

All-time periods

This system determines a fund's best, average and worse returns over various periods. These periods can have different start and end dates. By looking at returns over as many periods as possible over the fund's life, you can see the possibility, as a percentage, of losing money over any of the periods. You won't find this type of return listed in newspapers or other common sources of fund information. They are generally available only through mutual fund software programs, and even then not all of them.

Benchmark:
An index or peer group average against which to judge a mutual fund's performance.

Compare fund returns to benchmarks

A fund's past performance is more valuable when you compare it to an appropriate benchmark like an index or to the performance of its peer group. A peer group is a group of funds with similar styles and investment objectives. An index is a measure that indicates how the market as a whole is doing.

Since you are paying for the fund manager's skills and experience, you want the manager to add value by beating the return on the relevant benchmark. That means getting a higher return in an up market, and recording less of a slump in a down market. In reality, this is virtually impossible

MARKET BENCHMARKS

	Value	Simple rate of return % 1m.	6m.	YTD	1yr.	Avg. ann. cpd. rate of ret. % 3yr.	5yr.	10yr.	Std. dev 3yr.
Canadian equity									
M-Lynch Cdn. eq. fund index	1761.40	+6.6	-18.0	-9.8	-13.9	+8.1	+5.6	...	4.6
U.S. equity									
M-Lynch U.S. eq. fund index	2483.71	+7.2	-5.6	+6.3	+10.8	+19.6	+16.4	...	4.1
Foreign equity									
M-lynch Int'l eq. Fund index	1850.07	+10.9	-8.9	-1.7	-1.8	+6.5	+6.4	--	4.2
Bonds									
M-Lynch Cdn. bond fund index	1601.45	-0.2	+1.4	+3.8	+3.4	+8.5	+7.0	...	1.4
M-Lynch global bond fund index	1446.45	+0.5	+6.8	+8.7	+8.9	+7.6	+5.2	...	1.0

Major newspapers like The Financial Post publish benchmarks.

to achieve over any length of time. Higher returns in an up market almost certainly mean deeper declines in a down market. Always make sure to pick a benchmark that matches the kinds of investments the fund holds. And test your prospect fund against the benchmark over various periods. It's best to use a five to 10 year period and check both calendar returns as well as compound average returns. Benchmarks are also useful when comparing risk measurements such as standard deviation. Merrill Lynch Canada, a large brokerage firm, has developed mutual fund indexes that summarize average returns for Canadian bond, equity, U.S. equity, global bond and international equity funds. These benchmarks are published in business newspapers. You can use these to see how your fund is doing compared to the competition. Similarly, many newspapers, in their mutual fund tables, report average returns in

Benchmarks for Canadian funds

Fund type	Benchmark
Canadian equity	TSE 300 Index
Canadian large-cap equity	TSE 100 Index
Canadian dividend	TSE 35 Index
Canadian small- to mid-cap equity	Nesbitt Burns Small-Cap Index
U.S. equity	S&P 500 Index
International equity	Morgan Stanley Capital International EAFE Index
European equity	Morgan Stanley Capital International Europe Index
Japanese equity	Morgan Stanley Japan Index
Asia/Pacific Rim equity	Morgan Stanley Far East Index
Emerging markets equity	Morgan Stanley Emerging Markets Free Index
Latin American equity	Morgan Stanley Capital International Latin American Index
Global equity	Morgan Stanley World Index
Natural resource	TSE Sub-sector Weighted Index 100 Resource
Precious metals	TSE Precious Metals Sub-Index
Canadian bond	Scotia Capital Markets Universe Bond Index
Canadian short-term bond	Scotia Capital Markets Short-term Bond Index
Canadian mortgage	Scotia Capital Markets Mortgage Index
Foreign bond	Salomon World Bond Index
Canadian balanced and asset allocation	Combined TSE 300 Total Return Index (45%); Scotia Capital Markets Universe Bond Index (45%); and S&P 500 Index (10%).
Foreign balanced and asset allocation	Combined MSCI World Index (50%) and the World Index (50%).

various fund categories which also make useful comparisons. See opposite for a list of other commonly used benchmarks.

How to measure risk

When it comes to investing, most of us have a hard time defining risk. However, the industry itself has come to define risk as the odds that you will get the return you expect. Expectations are generally based on past history and anticipated future developments that might cause returns to go up or down. If a fund has consistently earned a 5% return per year over the past 20 years, you'd probably say the odds are high that it will continue to earn 5% per year. Although there is no guarantee the return will be repeated, the chances seem good that it will continue to do so.

But if a fund's annual returns fluctuate in a range from a negative -20% to plus 20% over a period of 20 years, what then are the odds that you will get a 5% return in the coming year? A lot less certain than in the first example, for sure. To calculate these odds, the industry has developed some statistical tools and measurements for an investment's volatility or risk. These let you compare funds and draw a bead on those that have a higher likelihood of getting you the return you want.

The more scientific measures used to gauge volatility include standard deviation and beta. You will find these measures in software programs such as PALTrak and BellCharts, in some newspaper listings and at sites on the Internet.

A simple, though less accurate way of measuring volatility is to look at the number of calendar years that a fund has lost money. You could also look at the difference between its best and worse 12-month periods.

The rule of thumb is to avoid funds with wild swings between annual returns.

Standard deviation

Each investment has an expected average return — but also a range of returns that are larger and smaller than its average. Those investments with the greatest range of returns — with the largest deviation from their own average — have greater uncertainty of returns in any future period. So those investments are riskier than ones with a lower standard deviation.

Standard deviation is the most common

Latin American equity

Invests primarily in common stocks and other equity securities of companies with principal business activities in one or more countries in Central and South America.

Fund name	notes	R fgn	% assets $mil.	Net NAV per sh.S	YTD distr. $	% simple rate of return 1 mo.	6 mo.	YTD	1 yr.	% avg annual compound return 3 yr.	5 yr.	10 yr.	Std dev 3 yr.	Exp rat %	L
Latin Amer. equity average:			42.5			+9.5	-32.7	-32.6	-26.9	+3.4	-5.4	...	+8.2	2.9	
Latin Amer. equity median:			24.9			+9.8	-33.3	-32.8	-28.7	+4.5	-5.4	...	+8.4	2.9	
AIM GT Latin Am Gth		96	14.5	4.93	0.26	+11.5	-37.4	-37.4	-29.5	+4.5	...	...	9.0	2.94	O
Atlas Latin Amer Val		100	8.3	8.62		+9.1	-27.4	-24.3	-16.7	+10.3	...	...	8.4	2.95	O
CI Latin American		89	120.4	7.62		+9.8	-35.2	-35.3	-31.7	-3.4	-5.4	...	8.1	2.83	O
CI Latin Amer Sector		89	12.3	6.37		+9.8	-34.8	-34.9	-31.2	-3.5	...	...	8.1	2.88	O
CIBC Latin American		82	8.1	8.78		+13.4	-33.3	-31.6	-29.1	...	...	...	...	2.70	N
Dynamic Latin Amer		53	6.9	3.41		+5.2	-30.7	-30.7	-26.8					3.48	O

Source: The Financial Post

You can check volatility in newspapers' monthly mutual fund surveys

Standard deviation by fund type

Fund Type	3 Years Median	3 Years Range
Asia/Pacific Rim equity	6.5	4.56 - 10.17
Asia ex-Japan equity	7.6	6.5 - 10.17
Canadian tactical asset allocation	3.24	1.66 - 5.33
Canadian balanced	2.87	0.8 - 10.45
Canadian bond	1.45	0.89 - 2.58
Canadian dividend income	3.5	1.78 - 5.3
Canadian equity	5.16	2.94 - 7.46
Canadian high income balanced	2.64	1.22 - 5.41
Canadian large-cap equity	5.01	3.73 - 5.77
Canadian money market	0.08	0.06 - 0.69
Canadian mortgage	0.65	0.55 - 1.6
Canadian short-term bond	0.67	0.27 - 0.92
Canadian small and mid-cap equity	5.64	3 - 10.17
Country specific	7.05	3.57 - 18.47
Emerging markets equity	7.21	4.7 - 9.07
European equity	4.08	3.71 - 5.34
Foreign bond	1.54	0.43 - 6.2
Foreign money market	0.02	0.02 - 1.82
Global balanced and asset allocation	2.64	1.78 - 3.73
Global equity	3.82	3.04 - 21.64
Natural resources	7.29	4.39 - 13.08
Precious metals	11.2	7.61 - 13.31
Science and technology	6.9	4.74 - 8.28
International equity	3.91	3.52 - 5.01
Japanese equity	5.68	4.74 - 11.66
Labor-sponsored venture capital	1.8	0.37 - 6.03
Latin American equity	9.71	- 5.19
North American equity	4.85	3.89 - 8.88
Specialty or miscellaneous	3.5	0.41 - 9.96
U.S. equity	4.16	2.85 - 14.19
U.S. small and mid-cap equity	5.41	3.39 - 8.31
Real estate	1.5	0.34 - 3.78
Unclassified	2.87	2.87 - 2.87

Source: BellCharts Inc. at Dec. 31, 1998

measure of consistency in a fund's returns. It is calculated using at least 36 months of a fund's monthly returns, measuring the variance of a fund's monthly return from its mean monthly return. The higher the standard deviation, the more volatile the fund's returns. You are after a fund with good returns — but also a low standard deviation. A low standard deviation over 10 to 15 years suggests the fund holds up well in bad as well as good markets.

You can find standard deviations for Canadian funds using software programs and on the Internet at the Fund Library and at GlobeFund. The Globe and Mail and the National Post newspapers measure volatility for mutual funds using simple High, Average or Low rankings based on standard deviation. The rankings are published in their monthly mutual fund surveys.

Beta

This is a measure of a mutual fund's volatility in relation to the market index it is compared to. Assuming the index is considered to be 1.0, a beta of 1.25 would indicate the fund is 25% more volatile than the index. Beta's value is that some funds might outperform in a rising market, but do worse when the market is falling. Beta for mutual funds is used less frequently than standard deviation. It is also used in conjunction with another risk measure called R-squared, which is provided in some software programs. You can get three-year Beta information on funds at the GlobeFund Web site.

Beta:
Tells you how widely a fund's returns deviate from the general market.

Does high risk mean high return?
The general thinking about investing is that if you want higher returns, you have to take more risk. However, a new study of mutual fund returns by the Canadian Securities Institute casts doubt on that thinking. It found that high-volatility funds generally don't compensate you with higher returns in the long-term. In other words, there may be no payoff for taking extra risk, so you're probably better off putting your money in low-volatility funds in a specific category.

Check what the portfolio is made of

Much of the focus of your research thus far has been on long-term returns and volatility. But a fund's holdings and tactics may change over time. Fund managers can alter the long-term composition of the portfolio or move heavily into a single sector for a short period. In fact, a fund that has good returns with low standard deviation may look like a good investment, but you cannot be sure until you have looked at the portfolio.

You will find holdings details in a fund's statement of portfolio, which is usually included in the annual report. As you peruse the portfolio, you will look for different things depending on whether it is an equity or fixed income fund you are studying.

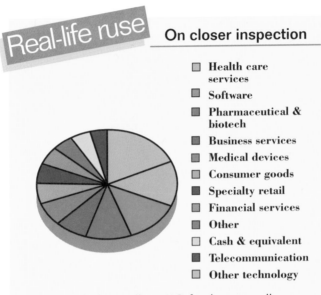

Real-life ruse — On closer inspection

- ☐ Health care services
- ☐ Software
- ■ Pharmaceutical & biotech
- ■ Business services
- ■ Medical devices
- ☐ Consumer goods
- ■ Specialty retail
- ☐ Financial services
- ■ Other
- ☐ Cash & equivalent
- ■ Telecommunication
- ☐ Other technology

At first blush this small-cap U.S. fund seems well diversified. But closer inspection reveals that it actually has 66% of its holdings in the volatile science and technology sector.

Equity fund portfolios

The first thing to consider is the portfolio's general composition. An important consideration is the proportion of cash in the portfolio versus stocks. High average cash levels — more than 10% — may indicate that the fund manager is having trouble finding suitable stocks to buy. High cash levels can also have a misleadingly positive influence on a fund's standard deviation. This is because cash assets fluctuate in value less than others and can reduce volatility from the stocks in the fund.

When looking at the composition of the stock portion of the portfolio, there should be no surprises, such as a high level of junior mining stocks in a

Big ten

Point of comparison

P/E Ratios and Dividend Yield for the 10 biggest Canadian Equity Funds compared to the TSE 300 and TSE 100 Indexes.

Fund name	Average P/E	Average Dividend Yield %
TSE 100 Index	19.36	1.93
TSE 300 Index	24.52	1.77
Ivy Canadian	15.15	1.98
Investors Dividend	18.24	3.17
Trimark Select Canadian Growth	N/A*	2.01
AIC Advantage Fund II	20.34	1.07
Investors Canadian Equity	21.1	1.7
Royal Canadian Equity	25.33	1.86
AIC Advantage	20.94	1.04
Investors Retirement Mutual	21.74	1.87
AIC Diversified Canada	20.98	1.06
AGF Dividend	19.93	2.29

*Not applicable. Stocks in fund, collectively, had negative earnings. Source: Portfolio Analytics Limited at Dec. 31, 1998.

large-cap equity fund. Beware of a fund that is overweight in stocks of one region, country or industry sector, unless you are buying the fund for this exposure. Also be careful of funds with high exposure to similar industries. Funds will sometimes break their holdings into separate categories when they could very well be part of one (see chart opposite). A fund with high exposure to one sector is riskier than one that's diversified across several industries. Portfolio composition summaries are available from fund companies' annual and semi-annual reports and at the GlobeFund Web site.

If you have a mutual fund software program, then you can also look at the average price/earnings ratio of stocks in the portfolio. Average P/E ratios higher than that of the relevant benchmark indicate the fund's stocks are higher risk. If there is a high cash level and a high average P/E ratio, then a low standard deviation for the fund should be viewed with circumspection. If the manager uses the high cash reserves to buy more of the same high P/E stocks, then the fund's risk-profile going forward might be higher than in the past.

You can perform the same analysis with other measures of value, such as average dividend yields of the stocks in the portfolio. The higher the average dividend yield, the safer the fund generally is.

Fixed-income fund portfolios

If you are buying a bond fund for income, your main concern may be how much and how often a fund distributes interest income. Distribution frequency is explained in the fund's prospectus. You can also get historic distribution details from free Internet sites like the Fund Library.

You may also want to check the quality of the bonds in the portfolio. Here again, the fund's portfolio statement will help. Funds' top 10 holdings are listed on software programs and at the Fund Library and GlobeFund Web sites. If it's high quality you want, then you will want to see a large proportion of Government of Canada bonds in the portfolio.

Effect of high cash levels on average terms

The high cash level in this fund distorts its average term-to-maturity. Even though 40% of its bond holdings are in long-term bonds of 10 years or more, and another 42% in bonds of more than five years, it records an average term to maturity of just 5.6 years.

Bonds				**Cash**	**Av. Mat.**
	%				
	Short-term	Medium-term	Long-term		
DST Bond Fund	18.5	42.0	39.5	38.7	5.6

However, bonds also have potential for capital gains and losses. You are effectively taking a position on the trend for general interest rates when you buy a fixed-income fund. This is because changes in general interest rates are the biggest determinants of how well most fixed-income funds perform. If you believe that interest rates are going to fall, then you would likely want a fund with a long average maturity. If you think rates will rise, then you'll want a fund with a short average maturity. BellCharts and PALTrak let you compare bond funds by their average maturities.

When looking at average maturities, it's important to remember that high levels of cash will shorten the portfolio's average maturity. This is because cash investments often have maturities between one and 12 months. You could find yourself looking at a fund with a five-year average maturity, only to find that the fund holds mostly long-term bonds of 10 years and more.

If you are simply looking for a bond fund to add stability to a balanced portfolio, then you will want one that has an even split between short, medium and long-term bonds.

Beware of changes in objectives

Now and again a fund company will change a fund's objective. This can be a major danger to you if a fund changes to a completely different objective, but takes its historic performance details with it. A Canadian equity fund that becomes a small-cap equity fund would likely have a lower standard deviation than most other small-cap funds. However, the comparison would obviously be unfair since the historic performance is not comparable to that of other small-cap funds. Details of historic objective switches should be mentioned in the prospectus.

Check for management changes

Investment management for a fund can be provided by a single manager or a team, and either in-house or through outside advisory firms. In some cases, particularly with foreign or specialty asset categories, fund firms use a combination of in-house and outside advisors.

Since you are basing your fund selection on long-term performance, it's important that as many of the ingredients that made up that past performance remain the same. While a new manager may continue the traditions of the former manager, the management change increases the chances of the fund failing to meet your needs.

However, the risk is less if the fund has been managed by a team according to defined investment criteria. A fund team that has found a successful formula is likely to stick with what works. Information about fund managers is often found in funds' annual reports to unitholders. However, funds are not obliged to inform you as soon as a fund changes managers. Fund manager changes are reported at the GlobeFund Web site and are also tracked by software publishers.

Weigh the fee and commission structure

Costs are something you should factor into your decision on whether to buy a particular mutual fund. If two funds have similar returns, equally low volatility and otherwise meet your needs, the one with the lower commission structure and MER is probably the one to go with.

But don't make costs the only thing you look at. A fund with a high MER, if it delivers above average returns, may be worth the extra cost.

Factor in tax efficiency

Like fund fees, taxes should never rule your investment choices, but they must be worked into

the overall decision. This is especially so if you are
holding funds outside a registered plan like an
RRSP. Mutual funds earn interest and dividends

distributions and do not take

Mutual fund dividends

Fund	Type	Amt.	Pay date	Fund
ABC American-Value	I	0.1281	Dec 31	Altamira
ABC American-Value	C	1.0030	Dec 31	Altamir
ABC Fully-Managed	I	0.0579	Dec 31	Altamir
ABC Fully-Managed	C	0.5772	Dec 31	Altamir
ABC Fundamental-Value	I	0.7333	Dec 31	Altamir
ABC Fundamental-Value	C	1.2116	Dec 31	Altamir
AGF Canadian Bond	I	0.0271	Dec 31	Altami
AGF Canadian Growth	C	0.8000	Dec 31	Altam
AGF Canadian T.A. Alloc	C	0.0750	Dec 31	Alta
AGF European Asset Alloc	C	0.5700	Dec 31	A

This column tells you if the distribution is interest or dividend income, or capital gains.

The Financial Post

from the investments they hold, and generate
capital gains or losses when they sell investments.
To avoid paying taxes, they distribute this money to
their unitholders to declare on their individual
income tax returns.

The amount of tax you pay is based on how
many units you own, and on whether the income is
interest, dividends or capital gains. Each is taxed
differently. Interest income is the most heavily
taxed of the three, while dividends and capital
gains enjoy more favorable treatment. You pay the
tax even if you do not physically receive
distributions, such as when they are automatically
re-invested in the fund.

To reduce unitholders' tax burden, many funds

pay their expenses out of the least tax-advantaged income before making distributions. This means expenses are generally deducted against interest income to allow for larger distributions of capital gains and dividends.

Some mutual fund software programs help you identify how tax efficient a fund is. You can also check tax efficiency by looking up the nature of a fund's distributions in financial newspapers.

Be aware that capital gains are usually distributed at the end of the year. This can pose a problem if you buy a fund close to the year-end. If you buy a fund with a NAVPS of $30 on December 1 and the fund has had a good year, you will be eligible for the capital gains distribution that takes place before the end of December. If this gain is $6 per share, the NAVPS will suddenly drop to $24. You may think that you've lost nothing after the $6 distribution, but after tax you will have less in hand. This is a reason to avoid making large lump-sum purchases late in the year.

Distribution:
A payment to you of interest, dividends or capital gains the fund has earned on its investments.

Stay on top of your holdings

Once you have selected your funds, you must continue to monitor their performance and other variables. Make a habit of reading your account statement, as well as the fund company's annual and semi-annual reports. While periodically checking your fund's performance in newspapers is a good idea, don't become fixated on daily changes in price. You are, after all, investing for the long-term.

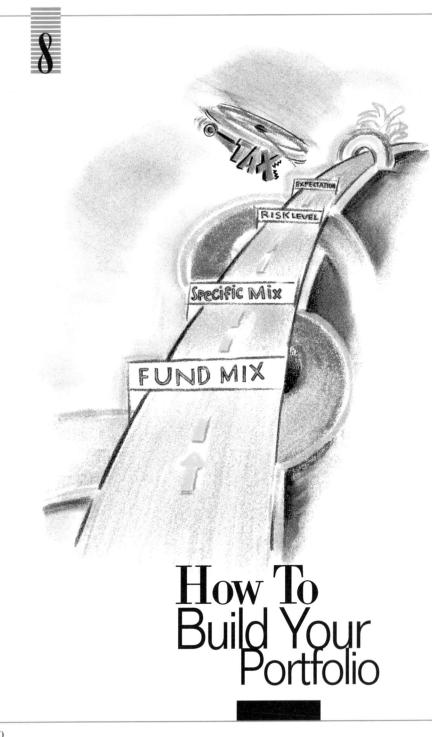

8

EXPECTATION

RISK LEVEL

Specific Mix

FUND MIX

How To
Build Your
Portfolio

S et your objectives, choose a mix of funds and keep monitoring them.

Write your investment policy

Writing a personal investment policy is a useful exercise to get you thinking about why you are investing and what your strategy should be. Think of it as your map for a long journey. It tells you where you want to go, how far you have to travel and the roads you will take to get there.

Your investment policy should detail your investment objectives, such as whether your main goal is to preserve your principal, earn income or grow your money through capital gains. You must also consider what obstacles could prevent you from realizing your objectives, such as how much money you have to invest, the time you have available, and whether you are comfortable with the level of risk you need to take to achieve the target you have set for yourself. It's important to set specific targets, such as to earn returns that are 2% above relevant market indexes or to earn income from your investments of $10,000 per year. Specific targets like these will direct you more quickly to the types of investments you need. You would never invest a big part of your savings in a small-cap fund that doesn't pay dividends if your main goal is to earn $10,000 income per year. Instead, you'd look at bond or dividend funds. However, you might find that to get $10,000 income, you have to buy a risky emerging markets bond fund. If you're comfortable with this level of increased risk, then a high-yield fund might be appropriate. But if the risk is too much for you, then you may have to lower your return expectations. This could mean investing a small portion of your money in the emerging market fund, with the bulk of it going to a lower-risk, lower-return Canadian bond fund.

Investment policy: *A set of guidelines setting out your objectives, constraints and return expectations for managing your portfolio.*

Your investment policy is not a static document. You will find that your objectives, return expectations and risk tolerance will change over time and with financial events in your life. You may be laid-off from your job or win a big prize in the lottery, either of which would be cause to revisit your investment policy. It's good practice to review your investment policy at least once each year.

If you have difficulty working through your objectives and risk tolerance, then you should sit down with a qualified investment advisor. Such a person is trained to identify your objectives and plot a course for you to achieve them.

Implement your asset mix

After writing your investment policy, the next step is to select the mix of asset classes that will help you achieve your goals. The three asset classes are cash and equivalents, fixed-income and equities. With mutual funds, these asset classes equate to money market funds, bond funds and equity funds.

Impact on your return

How you decide to allocate your assets is probably the most important decision you will make in constructing your portfolio. It's estimated that 80% to 90% of a portfolio's total return comes from your asset allocation decision.

The Asset Mix and Total Return table on the next page demonstrates the importance of the asset mix in determining your portfolio's overall return. In Part A, Ms. B outperforms Mr. N by 22% in cash, 100% in fixed income securities and 50% in equities. However, Part B shows that Ms. B emphasized fixed income securities and Mr. N emphasized equities. Part C shows the total return realized by each investor in a $1,000 portfolio.

Even though Ms. B outperformed Mr. N in each asset class, the asset mix decision enabled Mr. N to achieve a higher total return in the portfolio. So if you want to maximize the total return of your portfolio, it's more important to emphasize the correct asset class than to outperform an index or market average within an asset class.

Investment advisor:
A highly trained advisor who works for a brokerage firm and who is licensed to give you specific advice on investments to buy.

Asset class:
A group of investments that have common characteristics and which respond in a similar fashion to market changes.

Asset mix and total return

Asset Group	Ms. B	Mr. N
A. ANNUAL RETURN BY ASSET CLASS		
Cash	11%	9%
Fixed Income	8%	4%
Equities	30%	20%
B. ACTUAL ASSET MIX		
Cash	5%	5%
Fixed Income	70%	25%
Equities	25%	70%
C. TOTAL RETURN ON A $1,000 PORTFOLIO		
Cash	$ 5.50	$ 4.50
Fixed Income	$56.00	$10.00
Equities	$75.00	$140.00
TOTAL RETURN	**$136.50**	**$154.50**
TOTAL % RETURN	**13.65%**	**15.45%**

Determining your asset mix using the financial life-cycle

The amount of your portfolio devoted to each asset class is called your strategic asset allocation. It should reflect your investment objectives and your risk tolerance. A tool frequently used to help people determine their strategic asset allocation is the so-called financial life-cycle. The life-cycle has six stages:

1/ The education years are when you're going into debt on student loans and spending more than you earn. If you manage to save any money or already have some set aside, then your emphasis would be on earning income. Your asset allocation might be 10% cash, 60% fixed-income and 30% equities.

 2/ The early years are when you start a job, get married, buy a house, start a family and generally spend most of your money rather than save it. If you can save during these years, then the emphasis would be on a more balanced portfolio of 10% cash, 45% fixed-income and 45% equities.

 3/ The establishment years are when you are advancing in your job and starting to earn more than you spend. This is the time when you can afford to take on relatively more risk, so the emphasis will begin to shift to more of a growth portfolio of 5% cash, 40% fixed income and 55% equities.

 4/ The consolidation years are marked by higher disposable income. You start to pay off debts, see your children become independent and find you have more money to put into investments. With a decade or two still to go to retirement, you can afford to stress growth in your portfolio of 5% cash, 30% fixed income and 65% equities.

5/ The pre-retirement years are your peak earning years, but you are also nearing retirement so it will be time to start paying off any debts you may still have and to begin moving money out of higher risk equities to have a portfolio of 10% cash, 45% fixed income and 45% equities.

 6/ The retirement years are when your earning power changes and you begin to consume your accumulated savings. However, since most of us will live another 15 to 20 years, the proportion of equities in the portfolio will start out fairly high and gradually be reduced. The cash portion of the portfolio will become more important because of potentially higher emergency expenses. An early retirement portfolio might be one of 10% cash, 60% fixed income and 30% equities.

Select fund types

Having identified your asset allocation, your next step is to identify the fund types within each asset class. While spreading your investments over the three asset classes is one important way to diversify your risk, you can also diversify by fund type within each asset class to broaden your diversification.

Diversifying by risk profile

Funds within each asset class have different risk-return profiles. Two portfolios with exactly the same allocations to the cash, fixed-income and equity classes can have significant differences. One may be a high-risk portfolio that holds a money market fund that invests in higher-yield corporate paper, an emerging markets bond fund for fixed-income and a precious metals fund for equity. The other may be much more conservative and hold cash in a Canadian money market fund, fixed-income in a mortgage fund and equities in a dividend fund.

Risk differences in money market funds are based on the credit quality of the securities in the fund. In general, the lower the credit quality, the higher the yields should be. To assess these differences, you will need to look at each fund's statement of portfolio holdings, or you can use a mutual fund software program.

In fixed-income funds, risk will be determined by the credit quality of the fund's holdings and by their term-to-maturity. Longer average terms to maturity are generally associated with higher volatility, especially when the trend in interest rates changes.

Risk varies most among equity funds, but you can use four categories to classify funds of similar risk profiles — conservative, growth, venture and speculative.

• Conservative equity funds are primarily dividend funds, although global, international, European, U.S. and Canadian large-cap funds with higher average dividend yields would also qualify.

• Growth equity funds would describe most international, global, European, U.S., Canadian large cap and Japan funds.

• Venture funds would consist of small-cap funds,

emerging markets, Asia-Pacific Rim and resource funds.

- Speculative funds are sector, precious metals and country/regional funds.

By using differences between funds' risk-return profiles you can build a portfolio that more closely matches your personal needs.

Diversifying by management style

Much has been made recently about diversifying by management style, such as value and growth in the case of the equity asset class. There is conflicting research over the benefits of this strategy. There may be some benefit in the short term, but over the longer-term returns would appear to be similar between funds managed by different styles. A better strategy may be to select the management style that makes you most comfortable and stick with it.

Avoiding correlation

An important consideration is how the funds you select interact with each other. For proper diversification, you will want to pick mutual funds that are negatively correlated. This is a technical term for investments that tend to move up and down at different times.

A recent study by the Canadian Securities Institute gives some guidance on this point. The study concluded that:

- You need a mix of Canadian and international equity mutual funds plus interest-bearing mutual funds like fixed-income, mortgage or money

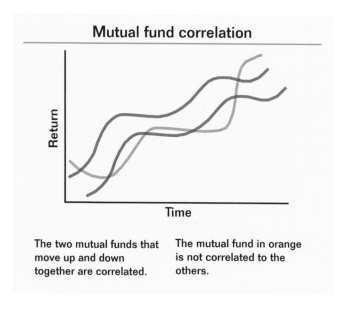

Mutual fund correlation

Return

Time

The two mutual funds that move up and down together are correlated.

The mutual fund in orange is not correlated to the others.

market funds for proper diversification;

- You cannot diversify between fixed-income funds since they all tend to move in the same direction at the same time;

- One of the only ways to diversify within a class of funds is in equity funds by adding international exposure.

Take taxes into account

You must pay tax on any distributions you get from a mutual fund and if you dispose of fund units for more than they cost you. If you hold units in a mutual fund set up as a trust, then you'll receive a T3 form at year-end. If your fund is structured as a corporation, you'll be sent a T5 form. These forms report all the income you received during the year, including reinvested

Negative correlation: *When funds tend to move in different directions in response to market changes.*

distributions. The types of income distributed — foreign income, interest, dividends and capital gains — will be identified separately because each is taxed differently.

Interest income

Money market, bond, mortgage and balanced funds most commonly distribute interest income. The amount is added to your employment income and taxed at your marginal tax rate, the rate at which your last dollar of earnings is taxed. So if you are in the 40% tax bracket, you would owe $40 in tax for every $100 of interest income. You keep $60.

Marginal tax rate:
The rate at which your last dollar of income is taxed.

Dividend income

Equity funds often pay dividends, which are taxed in separate ways depending on whether they are from Canadian corporations or from foreign companies. Dividends of foreign companies are taxed as interest, though you may get a tax credit for any tax paid in the foreign country. Canadian dividends are taxed at a much lower rate because dividends are paid out of after-tax money. You are entitled to a dividend tax credit. On $100 of dividend income, assuming a 40% tax bracket, you would pay about $25 in tax. You keep $75.

Capital gains

You pay capital gains tax in two ways: if a fund distributes capital gains to you or if you sell units at a profit.

When you sell your fund units or transfer between funds, you will generally trigger a capital gain or loss. If you have a gain, you must pay tax on the difference between your adjusted cost base for the units and the sale proceeds after any sales fees. This can become quite complicated if you have made periodic investments or reinvested any income, since you must make the calculation for your original buying price, as well as for every purchase you've made over time. Neglecting to keep careful records of original and subsequent buying and partial sales of units could be costly since you could end up paying tax twice on the same income. Most mutual fund companies give this information on account statements. If you sell a fund for less than you paid, then you will incur a capital loss that can be used to reduce any capital gains that you might have made on other property.

Whether you earn a capital gain by selling a fund or through distributions, you pay tax on 75% of the gain at your marginal tax rate. Assuming you have a $100 capital gain distribution from your mutual fund, you will pay tax on $75. In the 40% tax bracket, that works out to $30 of tax. You keep $70.

Consider holding funds inside an RRSP

Withholding tax: *Tax deducted by financial institution when you cash out money from your RRSP.*

Canadians may be heavily taxed, but the government has also given us one of the world's most generous tax-saving tools. It's called the Registered Retirement Savings Plan. There can be significant tax benefits to putting your mutual funds — and other investments — inside an RRSP.

There are actually two tax incentives for using an RRSP. The first is that you can reduce your income, and thereby your tax bill, by the amount you put into an RRSP. The government lets you contribute 18% of your income up to a maximum of $13,500. The second incentive is that any investments inside your RRSP are allowed to grow tax-free.

Self-directed RRSP: *Tax-sheltered account in which you can hold a variety of investments, including mutual funds, stocks and bonds.*

A tax wrinkle with RRSPs is that, when you eventually take the money out, you lose the dividend and capital gains tax advantage. This is because the amount you withdraw is taxed at your full tax rate. The institution where the RRSP is held must also withhold a certain amount of taxes on your withdrawal. When you file your tax return and calculate the tax you owe, you will be credited with the amount of withholding tax.

Of course, if you only withdraw your money after you retire, then your income might be lower than during your working years and you'll end up paying less tax. So you may still be ahead despite losing out on the dividend tax credit and the lower rate for capital gains.

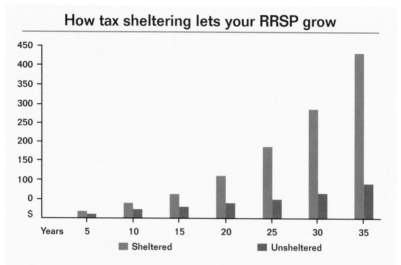

How tax sheltering lets your RRSP grow

Legend: Sheltered, Unsheltered

Based on $2,500 of pre-tax income being available for investment each year and a tax rate of 50%.

An average annual pre-tax return of 8% has been assumed.

If the $2,500 is allocated to an RRSP (sheltered), it is tax deductible, and the full amount is available for investment and all income generated is sheltered from tax.

If the same amount of money is put into a non-RRSP investment, only $1,250 of the $2,500 will be available for investment, since an equal amount will go to income tax. Also, all income generated will be subject to tax.

There's no limit to the number of RRSPs you can hold. You could, for example, open up a number of plans, each investing in different types of investments, with various financial institutions. There are drawbacks to having several plans, however. The paperwork can be burdensome. And it can be confusing to follow-up and monitor all of your investments. Most people have one or a few plans. You might have a group RRSP with your employer, plus a self-directed plan.

Monitor your investments

Once you've selected your funds, you can't sit back and wait for wealth to grow or for your monthly income to arrive. The ups and downs of the markets will mean you have to periodically rebalance your assets so that the proportions of equity, fixed-income and cash are brought back to roughly the percentages you want. By selling enough of those assets that have grown beyond their assigned allocation and using the proceeds to buy more of those assets that have grown more slowly, you will be selling high and buying low. It's generally a good idea to rebalance your portfolio once your asset allocation has drifted more than 5% from your strategic mix.

You also have to monitor your investments to ensure they continue to meet your needs. If your investment objectives change — and they most likely will — you will have to make changes to your portfolio. As you come closer to retirement, you should probably consider taking less risk and reduce your portfolio's equity portion and increase its fixed-income component. Remember, though, that equity funds will still have a place in your portfolio even after you've retired. This is because part of your money should continue to grow to preserve your buying power.

If you follow your funds' NAVPS in daily newspaper listings, remember that dividends and interest earned by a fund's investments are distributed periodically. Investors commonly use those distributions to automatically buy more units

of the fund. When distributions are made, the
NAVPS falls by the amount of the distribution. You
are just as well off as you were before that
distribution decreased the NAVPS. Your units are
worth less, but that's offset by the fact you now
have more of them.

Calculate your returns

The annual returns mutual fund companies publish
often don't tell you what your personal return was.
This is because you may buy funds part way
through the year or month at a price different than
what the fund company has used to calculate the
return. The simplest way to calculate your personal

Sample fund return

Amount invested: $1,000.00

Less front-end commission: $40.00

Purchase price per unit: $13.67

Units owned: 70.2267

Distribution received: $30.45

Current unit value: $14.90

Total return: 70.2267 units x $14.90

current value + $30.45 distribution

- $1,000 original investment = $76.827

or 7.68%

return is to subtract the amount of money you invested in the fund from your units' current value plus any distributions you've received on those units. If you paid a front-end load then the amount you invested is the full amount you paid, not the amount that actually went into the fund. The table on page 185 gives you an example.

If you are reinvesting your distributions, then the calculation is simpler. You simply multiply the total number of units you now own by the current unit value, then subtract your original investment from the total to give you your return.

How to choose a withdrawal plan

At some point, you will probably want to draw a regular income from your mutual funds. You can arrange to make withdrawals monthly, quarterly or at some other interval. Some funds have several withdrawal plans that let you withdraw some of your capital as well as any interest or dividends.

There are three structured withdrawal plans you can consider:

- A ratio withdrawal plan redeems a certain percentage of your holdings, usually between 4% and 10% a year. The higher the percentage, the more rapidly your investment will deplete.

- A fixed dollar withdrawal plan will pay you the same dollar amount each month or quarter. The withdrawals usually have to be in round amounts — multiples of $50 or $100. A fixed period withdrawal plan will withdraw the money each month or quarter with the intention of exhausting your capital within a certain period.

- A life expectancy adjusted withdrawal plan is a variation of a fixed period withdrawal plan. The withdrawals are designed to deplete your holdings by the end of your expected lifetime. To do this, mortality tables are used to adjust the withdrawals to reflect your changing life expectancy.

Maintain a long-term perspective

Although drastic downturns in stock, bond and other markets can be disheartening, or even alarming, historical data shows these markets bounce back. Equity markets have posted positive returns in most five- and 10-year periods, and all 15- and 20-year periods. What's more, as the markets turn around they tend to gain more than they lost during the downturn. Most of these losses and gains, especially in equity markets, are made in the few weeks after the change in trend, making it very difficult to know when to be in or out of the market. Studies have proven that the wisest strategy is to simply stay invested. This advice, of course, has to be tempered by your needs and circumstances.

Your success as an investor will depend on balancing your need for growth, income and safety in a mix of funds that take into account your unique situation.

9

Alternatives
To Mutual
Funds

Fund alternatives can offer lower management fees plus flexible trading techniques to enhance returns or lock-in profits.

Mutual funds are not the only way to buy into a diversified portfolio of stocks or bonds. A number of other products are similar to mutual funds, but often come with extra bells and whistles. These generally aren't widely known because fewer marketing dollars are spent on them.

However, if you're considering mutual funds, then you should also consider these alternative products. Many of them trade on stock exchanges and offer you the added benefits of flexible trading strategies that can enhance your returns or guard against potential losses. In most cases, though, these products are designed for specialized situations or for longer-term investment.

Pooled funds

Pooled funds are similar to mutual funds — but you'll need some serious money if you want to use these. A professional manager takes your money and that of other investors to create a pool that's invested in stocks or bonds. You hold units in the pool.

Pooled fund: *Like a mutual fund, but sold without a prospectus.*

Unlike a mutual fund, pooled funds are sold under the "sophisticated investor" rules where you need to make a hefty minimum investment — usually at least $150,000. Pooled funds are sold through an offering memorandum, rather than the prospectus used by mutual funds.

Pooled funds were originally created for institutional investors like pension plans, but a growing number of well-to-do individual investors are now using them too.

Lower fees than mutual funds

Pooled funds generally offer investors lower management fees than mutual funds. This is because of efficiencies created by the large sums involved, and lower operating costs since they pay no sales commissions or trailer fees.

The management expense ratio (MER) for

Canadian equity funds averages more than 2%; typical MERs for pooled equity funds are about 1%.

Since proper diversification requires you to invest in at least the three main asset classes — cash, fixed-income and equities — you would probably need at least $500,000 to create a properly diversified portfolio if you are going to only use pooled funds.

Pooled funds are offered by trust companies, investment management firms and insurance companies.

Segregated funds

Segregated funds, or seg funds as they are commonly known, are essentially mutual funds with insurance policies attached to them. Depending on the policy, the insurance offers a limited guarantee that you will get back at least 75% or 100% of the principal amount you invested in the fund. The guarantee only applies on your death or after the agreement ends, typically 10 years after you bought the fund. If you withdraw your money before the 10-year holding period is up, you will get back whatever is the current NAVPS. This might be higher or lower than what you originally paid. It's important that you understand this because the word "guarantee" has a tendency to give people a false sense of security.

Higher fee structure

The MER on many segregated funds is typically higher than for similar straight mutual funds. This

Median MERs for segregated funds

Fund Type	Median	Range
Asia/Pacific Rim equity	2.7	1.45 - 3.66
Asia ex-Japan equity	-	- -
Canadian tactical asset allocation	2.48	2.06 - 3.45
Canadian balanced	2.45	0.25 - 3
Canadian bond	1.97	0.36 - 2.49
Canadian dividend income	2.28	1.46 - 3.2
Canadian equity	2.55	1.04 - 3.24
Canadian high income balanced	1.86	1.5 - 2.41
Canadian large-cap rquity	2.41	0.67 - 3.2
Canadian money market	1.26	0.66 - 2.38
Canadian mortgage	1.9	1.5 - 2.4
Canadian short-term bond	1.72	1.44 - 2
Canadian small and mid-cap equity	2.4	1 - 3.42
Country specific	-	- -
Emerging markets equity	2.9	1.45 - 3.82
European equity	2.64	1.45 - 3.55
Foreign bond	2.38	1.63 - 2.76
Foreign money market	-	- -
Global balanced and asset allocation	2.79	2.12 - 3.1
Global equity	2.75	1.56 - 3.38
Natural resources	3.1	2.65 - 3.25
Precious metals	2.65	2.65 - 2.65
Science and technology	2.5	2.5 - 3.3
International equity	2.5	1.45 - 3.05
Japanese equity	2.13	2.13 - 2.13
Labor-sponsored venture capital	-	- -
Latin American equity	-	- -
North American equity	3	2.9 - 3.08
Specialty or miscellaneous	2.4	2.37 - 2.53
U.S. equity	2.55	0.67 - 3.25
U.S. small and mid-cap equity	2.6	2.55 - 3.15
Real estate	2.73	2.7 - 2.95
Unclassified	2	2 - 2

Source: BellCharts Inc. at Dec. 31, 1998

reflects the added cost for the insurance. You can expect to pay a higher MER on a seg fund with a 100% capital guarantee compared to one with a 75% guarantee. The insurance premium may add as much as 1% or more to the MER on an equity seg fund issued by a mutual fund company. Seg funds issued by mutual fund companies are often called guaranteed investment funds. Those issued directly by insurance companies are typically less expensive and compare favorably with traditional mutual funds. However, the loads seg funds levy are more variable. These have historically been higher than for straight mutual funds, and some seg funds continue to charge both front and back-end loads when this practice has been dropped by most of the fund industry.

Value of guarantee

Given the higher MERs and loads for many segregated funds, the question to ask yourself is do you need the insurance guarantee, and if yes what price are you willing to pay for it? Since equity markets have historically risen over the long term, the likelihood of actually needing the guarantee to get your original capital back after 10 years would be quite small. The chart from consultants William M. Mercer on page 194 rates the likelihood of making a profit in the stock market over various periods.

Of course, there is no guarantee that history will repeat itself in the future. As well, segregated funds guarantee all or a portion of your principal

Percent of time stock market has provided positive returns over selected periods

74%	83%	90%
1 Year	3 Years	5 Years

98%	100%
10 Years	15 Years

Source: William M. Mercer Limited

on your death. This can be advantageous should you die at a time when the net asset value per share of the fund has fallen below the amount you invested. Another advantage of seg funds is that if you have a named beneficiary, that person gets the money without your province imposing probate fees.

Reset features

Some seg funds let you "restart" the 10-year guarantee as often as four times a year, allowing you to lock-in gains you have already made. Of course, since the new value is only guaranteed 10 years from the date you reset it, this feature only has limited value, except if you die at a time when the fund's market value has fallen below the reset value.

Some companies will not let older investors exercise this reset option. If you have more than one seg fund, you may want to hold each in a separate account since some companies require you to reset your entire account. If they were all in the same account, you might be forced to lock in losses on some funds in order to preserve gains on your other funds.

Creditor protection

Protection from creditors is another potential benefit of seg funds. But you can lose that protection if you commit fraud by moving assets into a seg fund to avoid your debts. You also lose the creditor-proofing if your seg fund is in a regular self-directed RRSP or self-directed RRIF. You should consult your advisor.

If you are considering investing in segregated funds, you should be aware that the maturity guarantee might be reduced once you reach age 90. Some of these policies are simply not available to investors over the age of 80. You should also be aware that seg funds are allowed to publish their return statistics before management and other expenses are deducted. Seg funds are eligible as an RRSP investment.

Protected mutual funds

Another product offering a guarantee on your capital is protected mutual funds. These are not considered insurance products so probate fees are payable on them, and they don't offer creditor protection. Protected mutual funds, which come with terms of five or 10 years, can have significantly higher MERs than their non-protected counterparts.

Standard deviation for segregated funds

Fund Type	3 years Median	3 years Range
Asia/Pacific Rim equity	5.77	5.44 - 7.08
Asia ex-Japan equity	-	- -
Canadian tactical asset allocation	3.3	2.39 - 3.8
Canadian balanced	2.95	1.75 - 3.91
Canadian bond	1.41	0.96 - 2.17
Canadian dividend income	3	2.51 - 3.84
Canadian equity	5.14	3.03 - 5.9
Canadian high income balanced	-	- -
Canadian large-cap equity	5.1	4.43 - 6.02
Canadian money market	0.1	0.07 - 0.43
Canadian mortgage	0.6	0.49 - 0.99
Canadian short-term bond	0.65	0.65 - 0.65
Canadian small and mid-cap equity	5.3	3.51 - 6.52
Country specific	-	- -
Emerging markets equity	7.64	7.64 - 7.64
European equity	4.33	4.28 - 5.16
Foreign bond	2.01	1.54 - 2.37
Foreign money market	-	- -
Global balanced and asset allocation	2.1	2.06 - 2.29
Global equity	4.05	3.73 - 4.32
Natural resources	7.43	7.43 - 7.43
Precious metals	-	- -
Science and technology	-	- -
International equity	3.87	3.74 - 4.54
Japanese equity	-	- -
Labor-sponsored venture capital	-	- -
Latin American equity	-	- -
North American equity	-	- -
Specialty or miscellaneous	-	- -
U.S. equity	4.42	3.32 - 7.59
U.S. small and mid-cap equity	-	- -
Real estate	0.94	0.94 - 0.94
Unclassified	-	- -

Source: BellCharts Inc. at Dec. 31, 1998

Segregated, guaranteed and protected funds are extremely complex products. There is little in common between funds of one company to another. Before buying one of these products, make sure you get advice from a qualified advisor. And even then, make a special effort to read the fine print!

Unit investment trusts

Unit investment trusts (UITs) give you exposure to a narrow portfolio of stocks or bonds. While a professional manager picks the investments, the portfolio is typically fixed for five years. This can be attractive if you want to know exactly what securities you own, perhaps because you want to avoid duplication between your fund holdings. In contrast, if you buy more than one equity mutual fund, chances are good that there'll be some overlap in the funds' holdings, which increases your risk exposure.

When a UIT matures after five years, it sells its holdings and returns the money to unitholders in cash. Since UITs only rarely change holdings, there's little ongoing portfolio management, and therefore management expenses are mostly lower than for mutual funds. And while the trusts generally have administrative and marketing expenses, including trailer fees to salespeople, their MERs are still roughly 1% lower than for the equity mutual funds they most closely resemble.

UITs are generally marketed for a limited period of one year, after which the trust is closed to new purchases and a new version is set up with the same or similar holdings. Each trust has as part of its name the year in which it was established. As with mutual funds, you can redeem your units in a UIT at any time for their net asset value. However, UITs also trade on stock exchanges, which means you have the added option of buying and selling them at prices other than their NAVPS.

Equity UITs typically hold 10 to 25 stocks in particular sectors such as financial services or technology, which is why they should be thought of as a kind of specialty fund. In contrast, a diversified equity mutual fund might hold 50 or 100 stocks. Make a point of studying the stocks in the UIT portfolio to see if they are what you want.

UITs are typically sold with a front-end commission of between 1.75% and 3.75%. There is generally no redemption charge. However, if you buy and sell UITs on an exchange you will typically pay a brokerage commission both when you buy and when you sell.

UITs can earn dividends and interest, which result in annual taxes for you, although taxable capital gains are unlikely since the trusts rarely trade their holdings. Minimum initial investments are commonly around $5,000.

Closed-end funds

Unlike most mutual funds, which you buy and redeem from the issuing fund company, closed-end funds usually trade on a stock exchange. The price you pay for them depends on market demand and is often different from their NAVPS.

Closed-end funds are "closed" in that the

number of units issued is fixed and no new units are issued. In contrast, common open-end mutual funds continuously issue new units, which you buy or sell back to the fund company at precisely their NAVPS.

Only 20 or so closed-end funds are available in Canada. However, hundreds are available in the U.S. Trading information for these are listed in the Monday edition of The Wall Street Journal. Most of the U.S. funds traditionally focus on stocks from single countries. However, there are also regional funds and industry sector funds. Country specific and industry sector closed-end funds are riskier than regional funds simply because they are less diversified.

How closed-end funds trade

A feature of closed-end funds is that they often trade for less than their NAVPS. The discount reflects the market's view that the closed-end fund is a going concern, and is unlikely to be wound up and its paper assets realized at their then-current break-up value.

Closed-end funds are also more volatile than standard mutual funds. This is because they are subject to the vagaries of the market. Since they cannot be presented to the fund company for redemption, they are less liquid and supply and demand forces determine their prices. If bad news strikes a particular country or a region, investors may dump their shares of a relevant country-specific fund, driving down the price to a deep discount to

NAVPS. If investors anticipate a significant future increase in the value of the fund's holdings, then the shares may trade well above their NAVPS. A fund with a history of high annual distributions might also command a price greater than its NAVPS, particularly in a low-interest rate environment. Some closed-end funds also have a maturity date. As the maturity date nears, the unit price will tend to move closer to the NAVPS.

Buying closed-end funds

Since they trade on exchanges, you will pay brokerage commissions when you buy and when you sell shares in a closed-end fund. This is like saying they have both a front and a back-end load. However, being exchange traded typically means lower marketing and distribution costs for the fund, which translates into a lower MER. One prominent emerging markets closed-end fund that trades on the Toronto Stock Exchange has a MER of about 1.25% – half that of similar open-end mutual funds. If you were holding this fund for the long term, then the lower MER might well offset the front and back brokerage commissions.

Being exchange-traded also means you can use trading strategies like short selling on closed-end funds, which is impossible for ordinary open-end mutual funds. This lets you profit from a decrease in a fund's share price.

Managers of closed-end funds themselves have more freedom to use such techniques as short-selling. This allows them to hedge against adverse

Short selling: *Selling closed-end fund units in the hopes of making a profit by buying them back later at a lower price.*

market conditions and also to earn magnified returns on limited cash outlays. Closed-end funds can be held in your RRSP.

Index Participation Units

Index participation units (IPUs) are similar to closed-end funds in that they also trade on exchanges. However, they are also similar to index mutual funds because they're not actively managed and merely try to match the returns of a particular stock market index by holding a basket of component shares.

A major attraction of IPUs is that they typically have extremely low MERs. However, they're not suited for short-term investment because you pay commission both when you buy and when you sell them.

IPUs are generally structured as trusts and often pay you quarterly dividends based on dividends and other distributions the trust gets from the shares it holds. If the trust receives stock dividends, rights, warrants and other distributions from its holdings, it will sell them and distribute the cash to you. However, capital gains are kept to a minimum because the trust very rarely sells its component stocks.

Advantages of IPUs

- They have low management costs. Like index equity mutual funds, IPUs are passively managed, making them a cheaper alternative to actively managed equity funds. Not only do IPUs avoid the costs of researching securities, they also don't incur high administrative costs. The MER on the Toronto Stock Exchange's TIPS 35s is about 0.05%. This is a fraction of the cost of a typical equity mutual fund.

- They have a tendency to outperform most similar mutual funds. Research has shown that, in up markets, active equity fund managers have historically lagged the overall market as reflected by the benchmark indexes.
- They are easy to buy and sell. Since they trade on stock exchanges, you buy or sell them at current prices any time during normal trading hours. This is in contrast to mutual funds, which you can only buy or sell at closing NAVPS. By being able to trade at any time, you may be able to sell for more or buy for less than the closing NAVPS.
- You get broad market exposure and diversification. IPUs represent a simple way to gain exposure to a target market without the need to select individual securities. And because IPUs track market indexes, they represent core equity exposure, usually through companies that are representative of specific sectors.
- You have more trading options and flexibility. Unlike mutual funds, you can buy derivatives contracts called options or futures on most IPUs. You can use these to either speculate on the IPU's future price direction or to reduce your risk by locking in a price ahead of a possible decline. You can profit from IPUs if their value

drops since most qualify for short-selling, something you can't do with mutual funds.

Potential disadvantages of IPUs

• They will track downturns in the market. If the stock market falls, your returns from an IPU will drop along with it. Active mutual fund management, on the other hand, might be able to shift you into cash or take other defensive action to reduce your losses.

• They may not be suitable for short-term investment. IPUs trade like stocks and you pay commission when you buy or sell. For active traders, the cost of buying and selling IPUs could be higher than the costs of switching in and out of mutual funds.

• Their returns are capped. IPUs will only do as well as the market benchmark, never better. In contrast, an actively managed equity mutual fund has the potential to beat the market, though the odds are against it.

Types of Index Participation Units

TIPS 35s

TIPS 35 units are issued by a trust that invests in the stocks that make up the Toronto 35 Index, a market benchmark that consists of 35 of the largest stocks in Canada. The TSE 35 index covers the major industry groups of the TSE 300.

The value of each TIPS 35 unit is 10% of the

The TSE 35 companies

Abitibi-Consolidated Inc.
Alcan Aluminium Ltd.
Bank of Montreal
Bank of Nova Scotia
Barrick Gold Corporation
BCE Inc.
Bombardier Inc. Class 'B' SV
Canadian Imperial Bank of Commerce
Canadian National Railway Co.
Canadian Occidental Petroleum Ltd.
Canadian Pacific Ltd.
Canadian Tire Corp. Class 'A' NV
Dofasco Inc.
Imasco
Inco Limited
Laidlaw Inc.
MacMillan Bloedel Ltd.
Magna International Inc. Class 'A' SV
Moore Corporation Ltd.
National Bank of Canada
Noranda Inc.
Northern Telecom Ltd.
Nova Corporation
Petro-Canada Common/Variable Voting
Placer Dome Inc.
Renaissance Energy Ltd.
Royal Bank of Canada
Seagram Company Ltd.
Suncor Energy Inc.
Talisman Energy Inc.
Teck Corp. Class 'B' SV
Thomson Corporation
Toronto-Dominion Bank
TransAlta Corporation
TransCanada PipeLines Ltd.

index. In general, you buy and sell TIPS 35s on the exchange rather than buy or redeem them from the trust itself. This means you will pay commission both when you buy and when you sell, making these units best for long-term investors. Their trading symbol is TIP, and they are RRSP eligible.

The units pay quarterly cash distributions based on the dividends the underlying stocks pay. Expenses are deducted from these dividends before you get them. The MER for TIPS 35s is about 0.05%, a fraction of the cost of the average Canadian equity fund and much less than U.S. IPUs. You can learn more about investing in TIPS at the Toronto Stock Exchange Web site, www.tse.com.

TIPS 100s

These units resemble TIPS 35s but are based on the broader TSE 100 index. They were first introduced as HIPS (Hundred Index Participation Units) in 1995 but changed their name recently. The MER is about 0.05%. Each TIPS 100 unit represents 10% of the TSE 100 index. The trading symbol is HIP, and they are RRSP eligible.

SPDRs – Standard and Poor's Depository Receipts

Standard and Poor's Depository Receipts (SPDRs) are designed to track the performance of the broad S&P 500 Index in the U.S. They trade on the American Stock Exchange under the symbol SPY and are commonly known as "Spiders." Their price is roughly 10% of the S&P 500 Index. Like stocks, they are traded throughout every trading day. The net asset value of a SPDR is calculated each business day at the close of trading.

SPDRs investors are entitled to quarterly cash distributions corresponding to the dividends that accrue on the underlying stocks. Expenses are deducted from these dividends before investors get the distributions. The MER is approximately 0.18%, far less than the average U.S. equity fund sold in Canada. They are considered as foreign content in an RRSP.

Sector SPDRs

Introduced on the American Stock Exchange in December 1998, sector SPDRs let you invest in industry groups or sectors represented in the broader S&P 500 Index. The nine sector SPDRs give you an opportunity to focus on particular market sectors, from consumer services to the technology sector. Each sector SPDR pays quarterly cash dividends, which can be reinvested commission free in new shares. Ongoing management fees are around 0.65% a year, far less than similar sector mutual funds.

The nine funds are: Basic industries (Amex symbol: XLB); Consumer Services Sector (XLV); Consumer Staples Sector (XLP); Cyclical/Transportation Sector (XLY); Energy Sector (XLE); Financial Sector (XLF); Industrial Sector (XLI); Technology Sector (XLK); and, Utilities Sector (XLU). All are considered foreign content in an RRSP.

MidCap SPDRs

MidCap SPDRs were first listed for trading on the American Stock Exchange in 1995 under the symbol MDY. They represent ownership in the S&P MidCap 400 index and trade at a value of about 20% of the index. Unlike the broadly based S&P 500 index, the S&P MidCap 400 focuses on mid-cap companies, which may have more potential for growth. Expenses for the MidCap SPDR Trust are currently 0.30% per year, significantly cheaper than most small- to mid-cap U.S. mutual funds sold in Canada.

WEBS – World Equity Benchmark Shares

WEBS give you the opportunity to hold a representative basket of stocks for 17 different countries. Traded on the American Stock Exchange (see chart for symbols), the goal of each WEBS index series is to match the returns of the Morgan Stanley Capital International (MSCI) Index for the relevant country. Since the MSCI index measures a country's market activity, investing in WEBS can give you targeted exposure to a foreign country's stocks, without the need to make stock picks.

Each WEBS represents a broad underlying portfolio of publicly traded stocks in a particular country. Like foreign equity mutual funds, WEBS give investors exposure to international stock markets where it might otherwise be difficult to trade or even monitor holdings.

WEBS trade in U.S. dollars and each WEBS index series publishes its NAVPS daily following regular trading. This

WEBS	Symbol
1. Australia	EWA
2. Austria	EWO
3. Belgium	EWK
4. Canada	EWC
5. France	EWQ
6. Germany	EWG
7. Hong Kong	EWH
8. Italy	EWI
9. Japan	EWJ
10. Malaysia	EWM
11. Mexico	EWW
12. Netherlands	EWN
13. Singapore	EWS
14. Spain	EWP
15. Sweden	EWD
16. Switzerland	EWL
17. United Kingdom	EWU

means the shares often trade at prices close to the basket's actual value. Dividends and capital gains distributions are payable at least annually.

These are the 17 WEBS currently available (with approximate MER in brackets): Australia (1.33%), Austria (1.68%), Belgium (1.24%), Canada (1.35%), France (1.52%), Germany (1.37%), Hong Kong (1.43%), Italy (1.33%), Japan (1.19%), Malaysia (1.46%), Mexico (1.63%), Netherlands (1.46%), Singapore (1.43%), Spain (1.67%), Sweden (1.64%), Switzerland (1.52%) and the United Kingdom (1.38%).

DIAMONDS

DIAMONDS, traded under the symbol DIA on the American Stock Exchange, are based on the well-known Dow Jones Industrial Average (DJIA). The Dow is made up of 30 blue chip stocks traded on the New York Stock Exchange. DIAMONDS give exposure to the U.S. market, though the industrial focus of the companies that make up the DJIA means they don't offer as broad an exposure to American companies as SPDRs.

Units of DIAMONDS sell for 1/100th of the value of the Dow Jones Industrial Average. For instance, with the Dow trading at 7,000, each unit would trade at approximately $70. The MER on DIAMONDS is about 0.18%.

DIAMONDS pay monthly dividends to unitholders based on the cash dividends paid by the stocks in the portfolio, less fees and expenses. You can also arrange to have your dividends reinvested.

There are some possible complications you should remember about SPDRs, WEBS and DIAMONDS. The units of each trade in U.S. dollars. This exposes you to foreign currency risk if the Canadian dollar strengthens against the U.S. dollar. In the case of WEBS, there is an extra currency risk because the stocks in each portfolio will trade in their respective countries' currencies. Currency risk could wipe out gains you make in the foreign

Dow Jones Industrial Average Stocks

Allied Signal Inc.
ALCOA
American Express Co.
AT&T Corporation
Boeing Co.
Caterpillar Inc.
Chevron Corp.
Coca-Cola Co.
E.I. Du Pont De Nemours
  & Co.
Eastman Kodak Co.
Exxon Corp.
General Electric Co.
General Motors Corp.
Goodyear Tire & Rubber Co.
Hewlett-Packard Co.
International Paper Co.
International Business
  Machines Corp. IBM
Johnson & Johnson
JP Morgan & Co. Inc.
McDonald's Corp.
Merck & Co. Inc.
Minnesota Mining &
  Manufacturing Co.
Philip Morris Cos. Inc.
Procter & Gamble Co.
Sears Roebuck & Co.
The Walt Disney Co.
Travelers Inc.
Union Carbide Corp.
United Technologies Corp.
Wal-Mart Stores Inc.

market if the currency goes against you.

Remember that dividends paid by SPDRs, WEBS and DIAMONDS don't qualify for the Canadian dividend tax credit. Any dividends these products pay are subject to a 15% U.S. withholding tax. However, you can claim a foreign tax credit for this on your income tax return.

On a positive note, all these products can be held in your RRSP, subject to the 20% foreign content restriction. You can get more information on these products at the American Stock Exchange's Web site, www.amex.com.

Real Estate Investment Trusts (REITs)

Owning rental properties has long been a popular investment for wealthy people. With a Real Estate Investment Trust (REIT) you, too, can now own a piece of a property empire.

Structured as either open-end or closed-end funds that trade on stock exchanges, REITs use the money you contribute to finance the purchase of real estate properties. The rental income after expenses from these properties is passed on to you. Since Canada's tax laws allow REITs to deduct many expenses, they pay out a high percentage of their income to you.

Risks of REIT ownership

Before you buy a REIT, you should look closely at the trust's property portfolio. REITs can own different real estate types, or they may specialize

REITs often specialize in a particular property type like office buildings.

in one. Some focus on industrial properties, others on commercial office and retail space, and still others on sector niches like health care or retirement properties. A REIT with a variety of property types will generally be less risky than one that only invests in sports or entertainment properties.

Another risk is when a REIT's properties are centred on one geographic area. Property markets typically are impacted by regional economies, and a recession in one province or city could hurt a REIT if the occupancy level of its properties falls as a result. Natural disasters like earthquakes and hurricanes are another risk to consider because they aren't insured. A REIT with properties in several cities, regions or countries will be less risky than one heavily exposed to just one city or region. You can diversify geographically by buying several REITs with properties in different regions.

REITs must typically take out mortgages to

finance buying their rental properties. You should check to see what percentage of the trust's asset value is comprised of borrowed money. A leverage ratio of 40% or less is often viewed as good. Too much debt could expose you to the risk of the trust going bankrupt if it is unable to meet repayments.

Benefits of owning REITs

It's generally far easier to sell your units in a REIT than it is to sell a building. REITs that trade on stock exchanges can be turned into cash in three trading days. Open-end REITs are redeemed by the company within a few days of the NAVPS being calculated. In contrast, getting your money out of a building sale could take months. However, check trading volumes on exchange-traded REITs to ensure there's a ready market for the particular issue you're looking to buy. Specialized REITs typically trade less and are hence less liquid.

REITs also offer potential for capital gains, particularly in good economic times when interest rates are falling and the property market and general business environment are doing well. Even if interest rates begin to rise because of rising inflation, REITs are impacted only modestly because inflation increases their property holdings' values.

Most REITS can be held in a registered plan like an RRSP.

Index-linked GICs and structured notes

You can buy stock index-linked guaranteed investment certificates at banks, trust companies and investment dealers. These products give you the opportunity to make bigger gains than you might from a standard interest-paying GIC by tying returns to a particular stock index.

Some stock-linked GICs tie their returns to the TSE 35 while others are linked to the TSE 100. Foreign stock market indexes, or a combination of indexes from various industrialized countries, are also available as underlying benchmarks for these products.

If the stock market index tied to your GIC rises during the term of your investment, your return will reflect that gain. Unfortunately, many of these products pay you only a percentage of the gain, perhaps 80%. If the index rose by 25%, you would earn a return of 20%. Other index-linked GICs limit your return by capping your percentage gain, perhaps at 20%, even if the index rises 30% or 50%.

Some give you an opportunity to cash out early and take your allowed share of the gain. In that case, the original amount you invested stays with the bank until the end of the term you originally selected, and does not generate any further return for you.

Remember, too, that financial institutions don't use the total return stock index to calculate your return. They use the simple rise in the index and don't count gains from dividends paid by the stocks in the index. Some banks calculate the return by comparing the level of the stock index when you buy the GIC to its average monthly close in the last year of the term. That would work to your benefit if the market is falling towards the end of your term, but it would be a disadvantage if it were to rise instead.

GICs linked to foreign stock indexes are treated as Canadian content in registered plans, allowing you to increase your RRSP's foreign exposure above the 20% Revenue Canada allows. Taxes are another reason it's best to hold these products in a registered plan. All of the gain, even the gain attributed to the stock index, is taxed as less favorable interest income rather than as capital gains. And any gain is taxed in the year that it's earned, even if you don't get the gain in cash. Of course, this has no impact if you hold them in a registered plan like an RRSP.

Stock market-linked GICs might appeal to you if you want a shot at higher returns, but also want a guarantee on your capital. From another perspective, though, an index that falls or makes no gains means you get only your principal back. While this might not seem to represent a loss, your money will likely have lost some buying power because of inflation over the investment's term.

Total return index:
An index such as the TSE 35 that counts dividends and other distributions as well as capital gains on its component shares.

New structured notes

Some newer versions of these products, created

and offered by investment dealers, guarantee your principal, pay you a modest amount of interest and let you participate in any gains in an index. The range of indexes used is also more varied, ranging from returns on mutual funds to conventional stock indexes. In most cases, you are expected to keep your money invested for between three and 10 years before you will get all of your money back. An attraction of many of these products, often called structured or protected notes, is that they offer you international exposure that is treated as Canadian content in an RRSP. In general, though, the most attractive of these products are available only to people with large sums to invest — typically more than $100,000.

Some newer structured notes set the minimum investment at a much more manageable $2,500. These tie their returns to popular international mutual funds and are marketed to individual investors. However, these mass-market structured notes often do not guarantee your original investment. They also come with front and/or back-end sales fees as well as ongoing management fees. Their chief use is as a means to raise foreign content without affecting Revenue Canada's restrictions.

Hedge funds

Like mutual funds, hedge funds are professionally managed portfolios of securities. They have high minimum investment requirements, usually

Arbitrage:
The simultaneous buying and selling of an investment in different markets to exploit temporary pricing differences.

between $25,000 and $150,000 depending on the province where you live. For this reason, these products have been traditionally marketed to "sophisticated" investors. Rather than being only defensive in the face of possible market downturns, these funds are managed to make money whether markets rise or fall and actually thrive on volatility in markets.

In general, these funds differ from mutual funds in the range of investment techniques available to the manager. For example, a hedge fund manager may use such strategies as short-selling or arbitrage. While these strategies can be used conservatively, they generally carry more risk. Short-selling, for instance, lets you make potentially large profits if a stock loses value. But short selling also exposes you to theoretically unlimited losses since increases to the stock price are not capped.

Offshore funds

Offshore funds are based outside Canada, but are still subject to applicable securities laws and regulations here. They are sold through financial advisors or by the sponsor itself as private placements, with an offering memorandum in place of the prospectus.

Private placement:
When an investment is sold to a few buyers, usually institutions.

Offshore funds provide access to fund managers, investment strategies and particular securities generally unavailable through regular retail funds based in Canada. This lack of restrictions on potential holdings makes it extremely important that you review the offering memorandum carefully.

Like hedge funds, offshore funds may employ leverage, short-selling or hedging strategies that might not be allowed in a fund sold under a prospectus to retail investors. Since they are denominated in U.S. dollars or other foreign currencies, these funds carry currency risk. You could earn or lose money depending on what happens to currency exchange rates.

One advantage of these funds is their lower management fee structure, usually a result of being based in tax havens and of lower marketing costs to attract large investment amounts. However, for Canadian investors offshore jurisdictions can also mean less protection through securities regulation.

Offering memorandum:
The disclosure document used by offshore funds in place of a prospectus.

Wrap accounts

Wrap accounts are fee-based products that combine or "wrap" investment management, brokerage and reporting services into a flat annual fee, usually

based on the value of the managed assets. The fee would typically be an annual management fee of between 1.5% and 3% of the amount you have invested. Like mutual funds, one of the primary advantages of wrap accounts is the bundled professional investment management they offer. In comparison to mutual funds, wrap programs allow more scope to tailor holdings to your specific needs.

The major types of wrap accounts available to Canadian investors are:

• Mutual fund wrap accounts, which use mutual funds as their underlying assets. You would be paying fees on fees in this case since there's not only the wrap fee, but also the fees charged by the mutual funds. Typically, they require an investment of at least $50,000;

• Pooled wraps, which are similar to mutual fund wraps but hold pooled funds and have lower management fees. The lower fees are generally a result of the high minimum investment requirement. You're usually required to invest at least $50,000 in one of these programs. The asset pools available might be Canadian stocks, Canadian fixed-income securities, U.S. stocks or overseas stocks and fixed-income investments;

• Wrap programs that use individual securities, such as stocks and bonds. The minimum investment for these is usually about $150,000. They are offered through brokerage firms or investment dealers. They usually charge a fee based on the amount you are investing, with a certain number of "free" transactions included in the fee.

Epilogue

By reading this book you should have gained a more thorough understanding of investing in mutual funds and their alternatives. Of course, the investment business is never one to stand still. New products will continue to be introduced and variations invented for existing ones. This is generally good news for ordinary investors because it provides you with more choice and flexibility for your investing.

The trouble is that keeping abreast of new funds, not to mention changes in the economy and the securities markets, can be a formidable task. However, increasing numbers of people are finding this is not a chore but a source of enjoyment.

Managing one's own investments can be an empowering experience that instills in you a sense of achievement and self-reliance. If you're one of these people, then you'd do well to invest in a computer, an Internet account and a subscription to a mutual fund software program or a similar print-based service. These are widely advertised and offer similar information. Discount brokerages, the lower-cost firms that cater to the self-serve segment of the investor population, also supply a large amount of free information to clients. A recent trend has been the growth of online brokerages where mutual fund analysis tools are provided free to you online when you open an account. A typical discount brokerage offers you a menu of hundreds of different funds to buy. What's more, some will sell load funds on a no-load basis, which saves you even more money. Such incentives are the result of stiff competition between discount firms, so it's worthwhile to compare prices before you decide to open an account at a firm.

Of course, for other people it's one thing to know how to analyze mutual funds but quite another to actually do it. If this sounds like you, then the best approach is to seek the advice of someone for whom keeping on top of the economy, markets and products is a full-time job. Handing over the legwork to a highly skilled full service advisor will give you more time to do the things you enjoy, be it playing golf, puttering around the garden or going to a hockey game. Of course, after reading this book, you can now have confidence that the funds you and your advisor eventually select are ones that reflect your own best interests, investment objectives and risk tolerance.

No matter which approach you choose to take, remember that how you invest your money today will affect the standard of living you will be able to enjoy tomorrow. It is far better to take your time and be sure of your investment approach than to make rash decisions you will later regret. Do these things and you'll find that investing in mutual funds can be a pleasurable and enriching experience.

Mutual fund Web sites

If you're hooked into the Internet, you've got access to a world of information on mutual funds. The trick is to isolate useful investment information from the myriad of sites.

Staff of the Investor Learning Centre of Canada's resource centres in Toronto and Calgary have compiled the following select list of mutual fund-related Web sites. They've used their expertise and professional judgement to check the sites for comprehensiveness, content, analysis, ease of use, editorial content and timeliness.

Sites that contain Canadian information are indicated by a ❧. Bilingual sites are marked by the ⚜. As well, sites we consider to be particularly comprehensive get two stars. Don't forget to check out the Investor Learning Centre's own Web site — the Virtual Resource Centre — at **www.investorlearning.ca**.

Remember to type the site "address" exactly as listed. Some sites track usage by asking you for a *password*. Don't confuse the need to register and provide a password with the necessity to become a subscriber. Some sites offer a limited amount of information for free and require you to register and pay a fee before you can access more detailed information.

❧ BellCharts –
http://www.bellcharts.com

Features include the "BellScores": a ranking of Canadian funds by assigning between one and five bells, based on returns and correlation. The "Top Ten

Report" ranks the best performing mutual funds over 10 years, five years, three years, two years, one year and year to date.

Brill's Mutual Fund Interactive – http://www.brill.com

A complete set of tools for the mutual fund investor. Provides free quotes, portfolio tracking, news, corporate earnings charts, and Value Line fund screening.

✤ Canadian Ethical Investment – http://www.web.net/ethmoney

Recommends 15 Canadian mutual funds for ethical investing. Tables list their assets and performance.

✤ Fund Counsel – http://www.fundcounsel.com

The site includes some free information on mutual fund companies and investment strategies. Best of all is a "Battle of the Funds" comparison.

FundAlarm – http://www.fundalarm.com

A non-commercial (American) site providing objective information to help individual investors make the fund "sell" decision.

✤ The Fund Library – http://www.fundlibrary.com

**A comprehensive mutual fund resource centre providing company information, a personal fund monitor and portfolio tracker, a discussion forum and learning centre.

❧ Fundtrend – http://www.fundtrend.com

This site offers daily updates on the 60 and 100-day moving averages of most funds. The data is available in chart and graph form.

❧ Globefund – http://www.globefund.com

**Canada's national mutual fund site which provides reliable up-to-date and unbiased information, combines the Globe and Mail's mutual fund data with published articles from financial journalists, profiles of funds and companies and a learning section for novice investors.

❧ Gordon Pape's Web Site – http://www.gordonpape.com

Canadian investor information.

❧ Infofund – http://www.infofund.com

A personal online mutual fund monitor including over 8,000 U.S. and Canadian funds.

❧ Investment Funds Institute of Canada – ⚜ http://www.ific.ca

Ific's site provides information on industry regulation, investor education, and links to mutual fund company homepages.

Micropal (International Mutual Funds) – http://www.micropal.com

**Standard and Poor's Micropal is an international leader in the provision of fund information – monitoring over 38,000 funds around the globe.

Morningstar – http://www.morningstar.net

**Gives quick profiles for thousands of mutual funds, including NAV, annual returns and management information. Top 10 rating by SmartMoney, but fund holdings can be months out of date.

🍁 **Mutual Fund Dealers Association – http://www.mfda.ca**

🍁 **Mutual Funds Magazine Online – http://www.mfmag.com**

Thousands of articles on funds, hundreds of links to other fund-related sites and lots of tools for investors.

Mutual Fund Investors Centre – http://www.mfea.com

This site offers basic screens to locate funds with the lowest costs and minimum investment requirements, and a chart showing the benchmark indexes for various fund groups.

🍁 **Quicken –**
⚜ **http://www.quicken.ca**

Comprehensive investment site, including information on mutual funds.

🍁 **Portfolio Analytics – http://www.pal.com/**

The site contains fund summaries, quarterly reports and top 10 mutual fund lists.

Index

Notes

Notes

Notes